The Chernobyl Herbarium

Fragments of an Exploded Consciousness

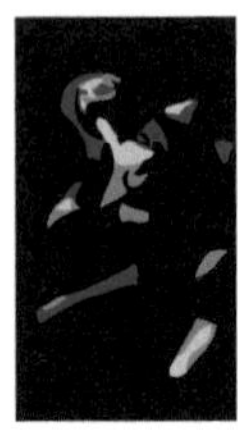

Critical Climate Change

Series Editors: Tom Cohen and Claire Colebrook

The era of climate change involves the mutation of systems beyond 20th century anthropomorphic models and has stood, until recently, outside representation or address. Understood in a broad and critical sense, climate change concerns material agencies that impact on biomass and energy, erased borders and microbial invention, geological and nanographic time, and extinction events. The possibility of extinction has always been a latent figure in textual production and archives; but the current sense of depletion, decay, mutation and exhaustion calls for new modes of address, new styles of publishing and authoring, and new formats and speeds of distribution. As the pressures and re-alignments of this re-arrangement occur, so must the critical languages and conceptual templates, political premises and definitions of 'life.' There is a particular need to publish in timely fashion experimental monographs that redefine the boundaries of disciplinary fields, rhetorical invasions, the interface of conceptual and scientific languages, and geomorphic and geopolitical interventions. Critical Climate Change is oriented, in this general manner, toward the epistemo-political mutations that correspond to the temporalities of terrestrial mutation.

The Chernobyl Herbarium

Fragments of an Exploded Consciousness

Michael Marder
with artworks by *Anaïs Tondeur*

()
OPEN HUMANITIES PRESS
London 2016

First edition published by OPEN HUMANITIES PRESS 2016

ISBN (print) 978-1-78542-026-9
ISBN (pdf) 978-1-78542-027-6

OPEN HUMANITIES PRESS

OPEN HUMANITIES PRESS is an international, scholar-led open access publishing collective whose mission is to make leading works of contemporary critical thought freely available worldwide. More at http://openhumanitiespress.org

Contents

Эта книга посвящается земле, животным, воде, людям, воздуху и растениям, пострадавшим от Чернобыльской катастрофы

Ця книга присвячується землі, тваринам, воді, людям, повітрю і рослинам, постраждалим від Чорнобильської катастрофи

Гэтая кніга прысвячаецца зямлі, жывёлам, вадзе, людзям, паветры і раслінам, якія пацярпелі ад Чарнобыльскай катастрофы

Chernobyl exploded my brain. I started thinking.

Oleg Vorobey, liquidator; quoted in Svetlana Alexievich, *Voices from Chernobyl*

And that was why, he'd say, stroking his black hair as if stroking the soft, hot fur of a kitten, that was why his life amounted to a pile of shards: some shiny, others clouded, some cheerful, others like a "piece of a wasted hour," meaningless, some red and full, others white, but already shattered.

Clarice Lispector, "Interrupted Story"

Keep my shadow. I cannot explain. Sorry.
It needs to be done now. Keep my shadow. Keep it.

Joseph Brodsky, "Letters to a Wall"

Preface

We entrust readers with thirty fragments of reflections, meditations, recollections, and images—one for each year that has passed since the explosion that rocked and destroyed a part of the Chernobyl nuclear power station in April 1986. The aesthetic visions, thoughts, and experiences that have made their way into this book hover in a grey region between the singular and self-enclosed, on the one hand, and the generally applicable and universal, on the other. They are the splinters of what, inspired by Svetlana Alexievich's *Voices from Chernobyl*, we call *an exploded consciousness*. As the author says about the not-so-evident effects of Chernobyl in an interview with herself, ventriloquizing in the same breath the testimony of Oleg Vorobey, a "liquidator" of the meltdown's consequences: "It was a catastrophe of consciousness. The world of our conceptions and values has exploded."[1] Sure: it signaled the demise of the collective Soviet subject, which coincided with and accelerated the collapse of the Soviet Union. More broadly construed, it was also a trauma of European and planetary proportions that weakened the already waning faith in technological progress and the illusion of security cherished within the borders of affluent nation-states.

What of this event remains today, in 2016? Both too much and too little.

Too much, because thirty years is an insignificant stretch of time, a blip in a chronology that will take centuries for the affected soil and natural environment to be decontaminated. And because the survivors and their children continue developing health problems and dying due to external and internal (diet-related) radiation exposure.

Too little, because the trauma of Chernobyl has not been worked through in the absence of a consciousness appropriate to the task of representing it. Nuclear power production in Europe and around the world has not been halted, and some even dare to claim that it is safer and more environmentally sound than that obtained by burning fossil fuels. A fundamental rethinking of the meaning of energy and its procurement is yet to take place against the dual backdrop of Chernobyl (and now Fukushima) and human-induced climate change.

Our wager in this small book is to contribute our humble share to a collaborative grappling with the event of Chernobyl. Unthinkable and unrepresentable as it is, we insist on the need to reflect upon, signify, and symbolize it, taking stock of the consciousness it fragmented and, perhaps, cultivating another, more environmentally attuned way of living.

We are also keenly aware that we are endeavoring to think the unthinkable and represent the unrepresentable. Hence the paths we have chosen: in lieu of dispassionate argumentation, you will find here meditations on personal experiences, aesthetic objects, and political processes; in lieu of photographs or paintings, you will view photograms, created through the direct imprints of radioactive herbarium specimens, grown in the soil of "the exclusion zone" by Martin Hajduch of the Institute of Plant Genetics and Biotechnology at the Slovak Academy of Sciences and arranged on photosensitive paper. As always, plants will be our guides, reconnecting us with the (hopelessly contaminated) soil, illuminating the meaning of the remains, and helping us to envision a kind of testimony that respects absolute silence.

Michael Marder (Vitoria-Gasteiz, Spain) &
Anaïs Tondeur (Montreuil, France) – January 2016

Fragment 1 **Train station**

It's April 26, 1986. I am on a sleeper train, traveling from Moscow to the town of Anapa, located in Southern Russia, on the shore of the Black Sea. I have been aboard one of the cars for nearly two days and the provisions we had brought from home are running out. The train is stopped in Rostov-on-Don, a thousand and two hundred kilometers away from the city where I live. From my upper-level bed, I look out the window and a lively scene is unfolding before my eyes: the hustle and bustle typical of a central station; older ladies selling hot meat- and potato-pies, fried chicken, and pickles; people rushing in and out of the train. No one has any idea about what is going on eight hundred kilometers northwest. That is the true meaning of an event: it happens without us awakening to it, that is, it happens as though it did not happen, confined to the thing itself, in the thing itself, which nonetheless includes us, enfolds us, gathers us into its assembly, asking us not whether we wish to be included. Radioactive fallout clouds from Chernobyl and the official information about the incident, the one a distorted mirror reflection of the other, have not reached us yet, and they will not do so for some days. But the event is afoot. It will catch up with us, before we have a chance to catch up with it, if at all. In the meantime, life will continue to wind through its "normal" course. I am espying its ebbs and flows on the Rostov-on-Don platform, from inside the train compartment, in which I am traveling.

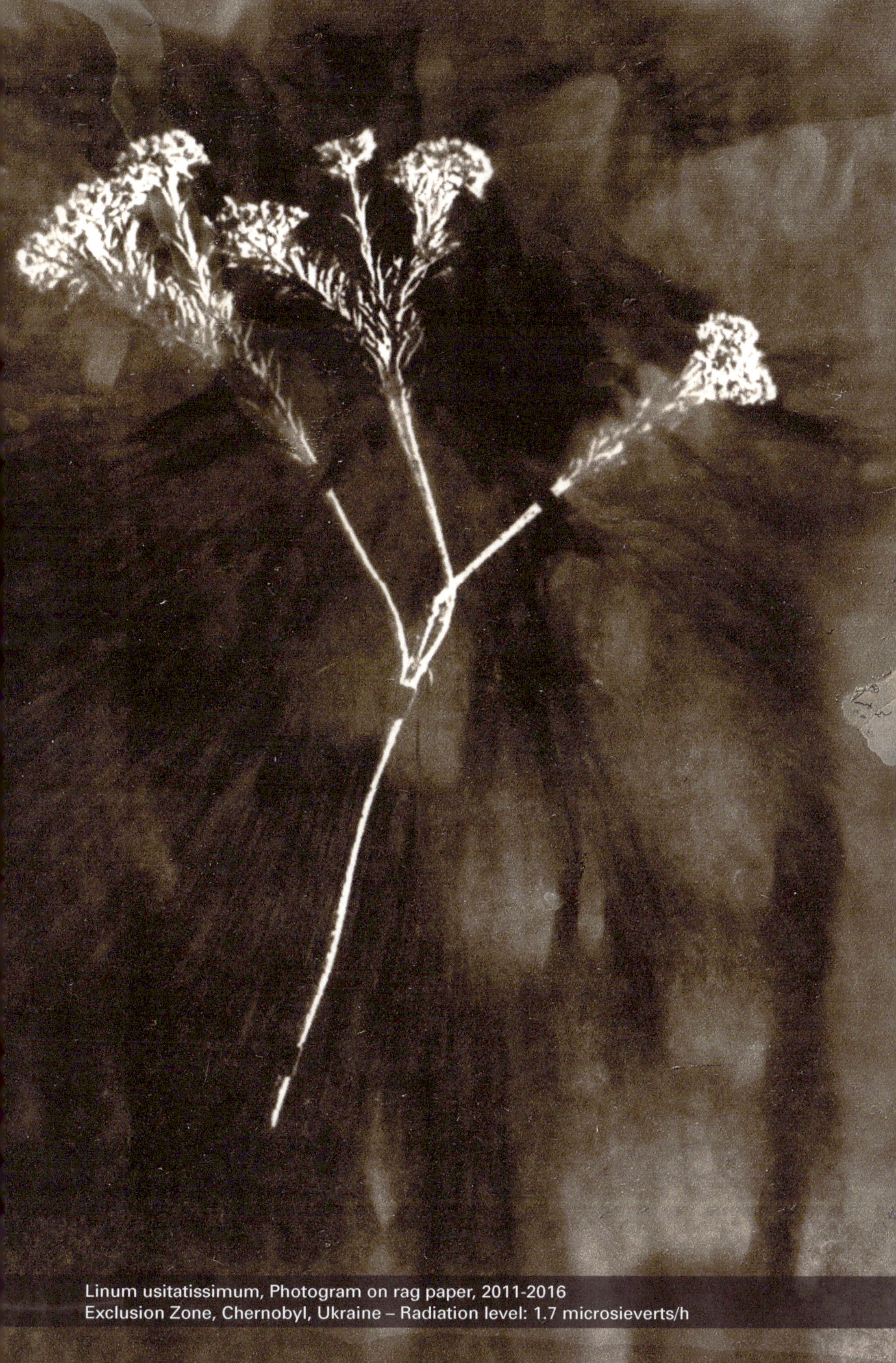

Linum usitatissimum, Photogram on rag paper, 2011-2016
Exclusion Zone, Chernobyl, Ukraine – Radiation level: 1.7 microsieverts/h

Fragment 2 **Explosions of light**

Some images in Anaïs Tondeur's Chernobyl Herbarium are the explosions of light. Others are softly glowing, breathing with fragility and precariousness. The explosive imprints are, in effect, reminiscent of volcanic eruptions at night, hot lava spewing from the depths of the earth. Even assuming it is not an actual trace of radiation (which the specimens in the herbarium have received from the isotopes of cesium-137 and strontium-90 mixed with the soil of the exclusion zone) that comes through and shines forth from the plants' contact with photosensitive paper, the resulting works of art cannot help but send us back to a space and time outside the frame, wherein this *Linum usitatissimum* germinated, grew, and blossomed.

The images are the visible records of an invisible calamity, tracked across the threshold of sight by the power of art. The literal translation from Greek of the technique used here, *photogram*, is a *line of light*. Not a *photograph*, the *writing of light*, but a photogram, its line captured on photosensitive paper, upon which the object is placed. In writing, a line is already too idealized, too heavy with meaning, overburdened with sense, nearly immaterial. In a photograph, light's imprint is further removed from the being that emitted or reflected it than in a photogram, where, absent the camera, the line can be itself, can trace itself outside the system of coded significations and machinic mediations. The *grammé* of a photogram imposes itself from up close. Touching... It endures: etched, engraved, engrained, the energy it transported both reflected (or refracted) *and* absorbed. Much like radiation, indifferently imbibed by whatever and whoever is on its path—the soil, buildings, plants, animals, humans—yet uncontainable in any single entity whose time-frame it invariably overflows. Through her aesthetic practice, Tondeur detonates, releases the explosions of light trapped in plants, its lines dispersed, crisscrossing photograms every which way. She liberates luminescent traces without violence, avoiding the repetition of the first, invisible event of Chernobyl and, at the same time, capturing something of it. Release and preservation; preservation and release: by the grace of art.

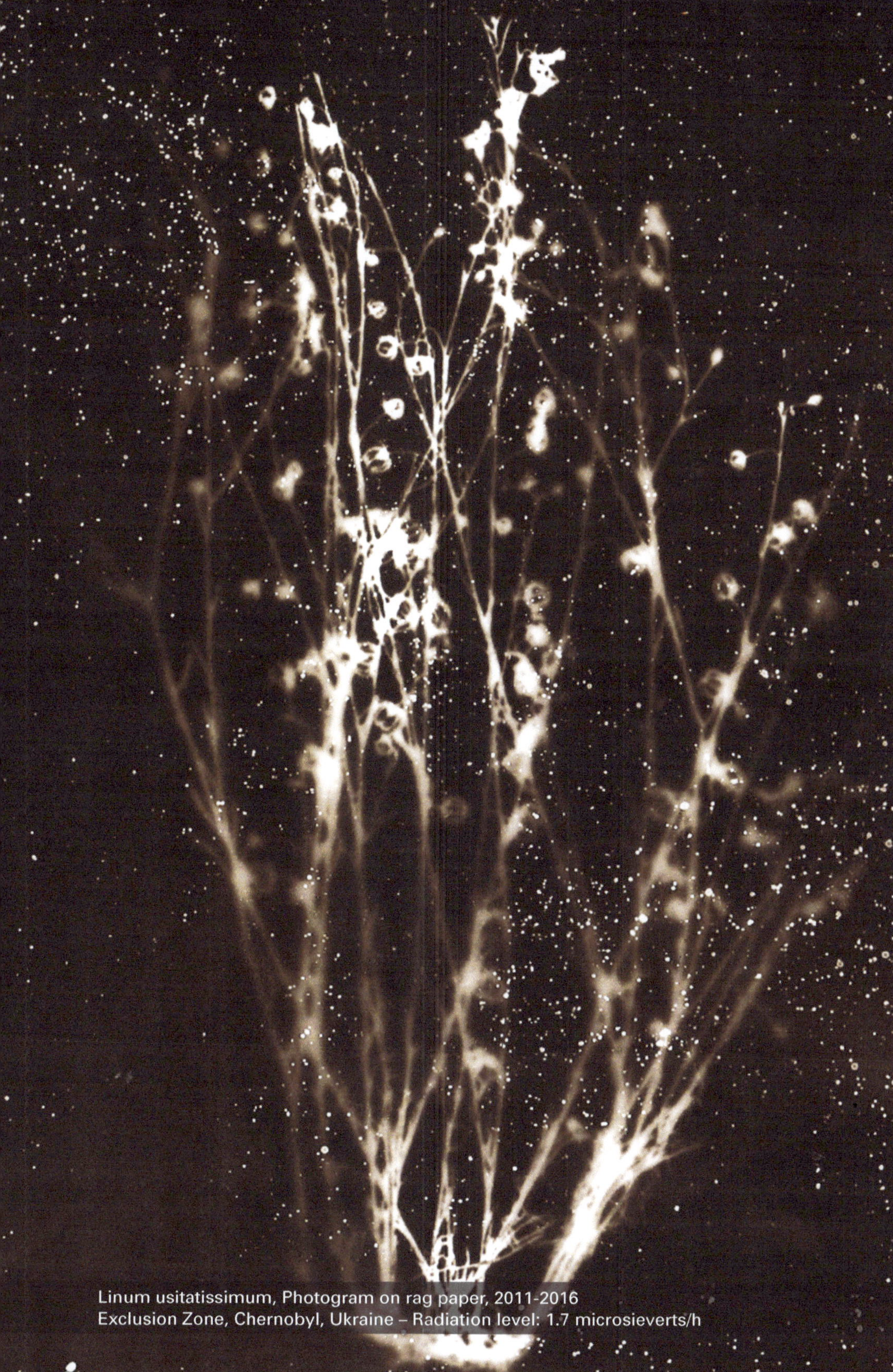

Linum usitatissimum, Photogram on rag paper, 2011-2016
Exclusion Zone, Chernobyl, Ukraine – Radiation level: 1.7 microsieverts/h

Fragment 3 **We flee toward the thing we try to escape**

Why was I heading south in late April 1986 for the first time in what will have become my strange annual pilgrimage, in the company of a parent, over the subsequent three years? This trip, like the ones to come (again to Anapa in 1987 and, later, still further away, to the city of Sukhumi in the Abkhazia region of the former Soviet Republic of Georgia) was an escape, mandated by doctors and sponsored by the healthcare system of the USSR. As a result of severe seasonal allergies to birch, oak, and other tree pollen, which left me breathless, the medical decision was to send me to "another climactic zone," where none of the vegetation prevalent in Central European Russia flourished.

I thus had to spend a part of the spring among palm trees and cypresses, transplanted. The reason for this predicament, shared to a lesser degree with the majority of my peers, was clear: on the outskirts of Moscow, my apartment block was situated between a massive forest and a large, air-polluting factory. As I recount in *Through Vegetal Being*: "depending on the direction of the wind, we sensed either the smell of fumes that emanated from the industrial monstrosity or fresh air that drifted from the woods."[2] In a roundabout way, I was cut off from the world of vegetation at the time of its renewal by the unchecked forces of industrialization and a dangerously naïve ideology of progress, as prevalent in the Soviet Union as it was in the West. And this means that my medically recommended escape had to do with the technological domination of the natural environment that made the world unbearable and ultimately unlivable.

But the impression that one can flee from the calamity that is our civilization is no less immature than the sunny ideology of progress itself. There are no escape valves. By train, I was speeding toward another, still greater catastrophe spawned by the same total system (I am not alluding to Soviet "totalitarianism" but to the pernicious ubiquity of an instrumental handling of nature that undercuts life and prevails both in capitalist and socialist economic systems). Breathing freely, no longer afflicted by allergy-induced asthma, I will spend the rest of April, May, and a part of June on the shores of the Black Sea, where, unbeknownst to me, I will be receiving dangerous amounts of radiation from Chernobyl's fallout. Jean Baudrillard dubs this *the logic of seduction*, of fleeing toward the thing we are trying to escape. The seduction of technology? Of being human? Or are these altogether interchangeable?

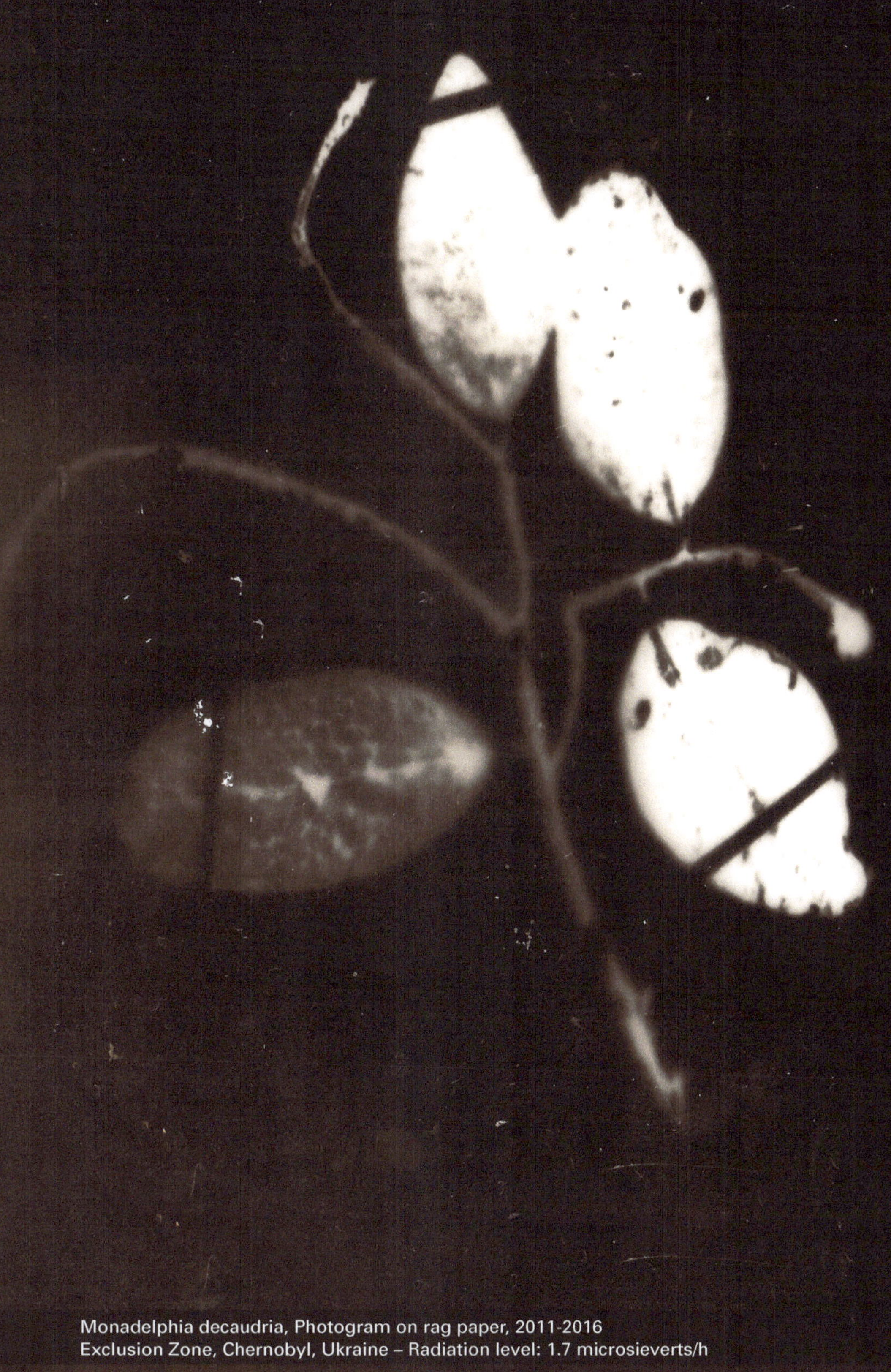

Monadelphia decaudria, Photogram on rag paper, 2011-2016
Exclusion Zone, Chernobyl, Ukraine – Radiation level: 1.7 microsieverts/h

Fragment 4 **The extraordinary nature of the ordinary**

Usually, when philosophers and artists illuminate the extraordinary nature of ordinary phenomena, they do so by pointing out an unexpected conceptual or aesthetic angle on everyday, taken-for-granted things. For instance, they wrest objects from the familiar contexts of their routine use, as Duchamp did with the urinal titled *Fountain* in 1917, or they see portions of reality as examples of metaphysical ideas, as Hegel did in the nineteenth century when he interpreted even "ordinary actuality"—the air and the earth, the family and the state ... —as the avatars of Spirit.

These are not the appropriate illustrations of the extraordinariness of the ordinary I have in mind. I am thinking, above all, of the false façade of calm and unremarkably habitual existence in the aftermath of the Chernobyl accident: in the immediate surroundings of the nuclear power station prior to mass evacuations; in Kiev and Minsk where May 1 demonstrations went ahead as scheduled; and in further removed fallout areas, such as Anapa, where, according to official figures, in early May 1986 radiation readings reached 60 mR/hr (milliRoentgens per hour),[3] a value some 300 times higher than the "normal" levels of 0.2 mR/hr. The invisibility of giant doses of radiation was doubled up, covered over, and magnified by the political obfuscation of the disaster, the full scope of which started to emerge only when abnormally elevated readings were detected in Sweden two days after the release of radioactive debris into the atmosphere. No earlier than on May 6 and 7 did the newspaper *Pravda* provide extensive reports on the accident.

Unperceivable and unannounced, the event of Chernobyl with its wide repercussions was, right after it happened, indistinguishable from the course of everyday life. The state of exception it provoked was not exceptional, from the standpoint of whoever lived through it. Everything was changed unnoticed and unnoted, at least initially. (The same actually applies to the collapse of the Soviet Union that swiftly followed that of Chernobyl.) The atmosphere, air, water, soil, plants, animals, people—all that seemed to be exactly the same as yesterday, in spite of being radically transformed. It is when things are in the clear, at their most obvious and mundane, that they are totally obscure, relegated to the dark by our own sense of obviousness and absolute clarity. The sole exciting thing for the six-year-old that I was consisted in being, for the first time in his life, by the seaside, in what appeared to be a warm paradise, with its pebble beaches and occasional evergreen vegetation.

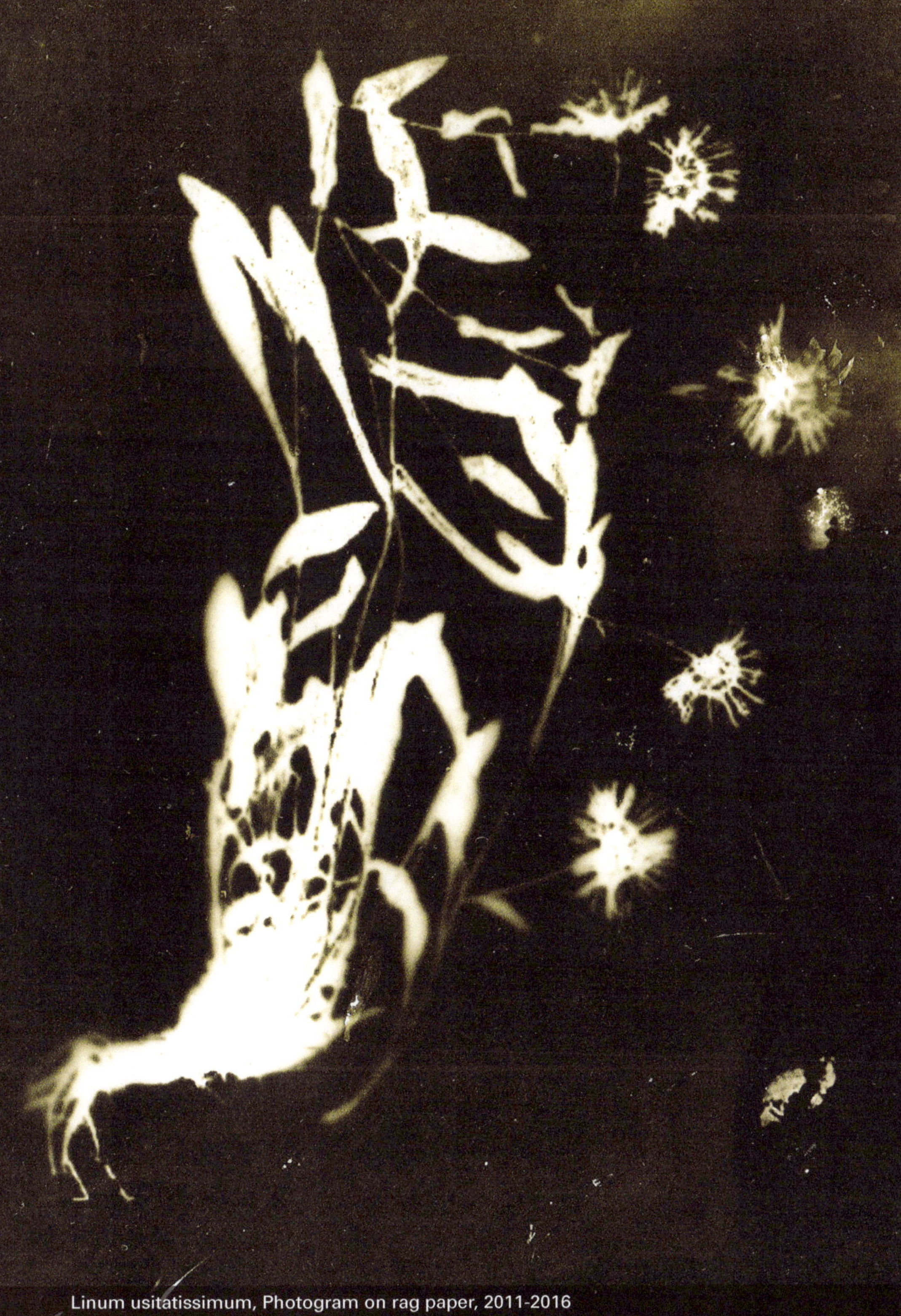

Linum usitatissimum, Photogram on rag paper, 2011-2016
Exclusion Zone, Chernobyl, Ukraine – Radiation level: 1.7 microsieverts/h

Fragment 5 **Meaning's excess**

Before we consume, burn, decorate and pay tributes with, or contemplate them, plants irradiate a meaning of their own. Each branch, shoot, and leaf located in a particular portion of a geranium, or of any other plant, is the outcome of a lived vegetal interpretation of the environment: the direction and intensity of sunlight, the amount of moisture in the air, and so forth. Plants' living forms are *their* semantic structures. The human production of meaning is inevitably belated, supplementary, superadded to whatever we interpret, though, from our perspective, it stands out as the essential (in effect, the only) semantic construction.

The geranium, then, shines forth, gives itself to sight and to the other senses by unfurling its leaves and flowers in a uniquely vegetal mode of exposure intended to maximize the amount of sunlight it receives. In Tondeur's herbarium, it does not light up as explosively, shockingly, and unsustainably as *Linum usitatissumum*[4] but emanates a steady glow, similar to the continuous acts of meaning-making by living plants, the acts coextensive with their lives. For the plant, the ongoing monitoring of environmental conditions in the place of its growth is a run-of-the-mill operation; for us, who are accustomed to thinking of plants as passive beings devoid of consciousness or as persisting in a state of torpor at best, it is extraordinary.

There is also, in Tondeur's plants, an excess of meaning, untethered to cultural, scientific, or other human constructions and related, instead, to the history of their growth in radioactive soil. That is the additional shimmer behind the shining—visual and semantic—vegetal imprint. Together with radioactivity, the plant whose trace we are contemplating assimilated the imperceptible and the inconceivable that, at the edge of sense, jump at us from the photogram. Its excess of meaning is dense, impenetrable. In the thick of infinite openness and exposure.

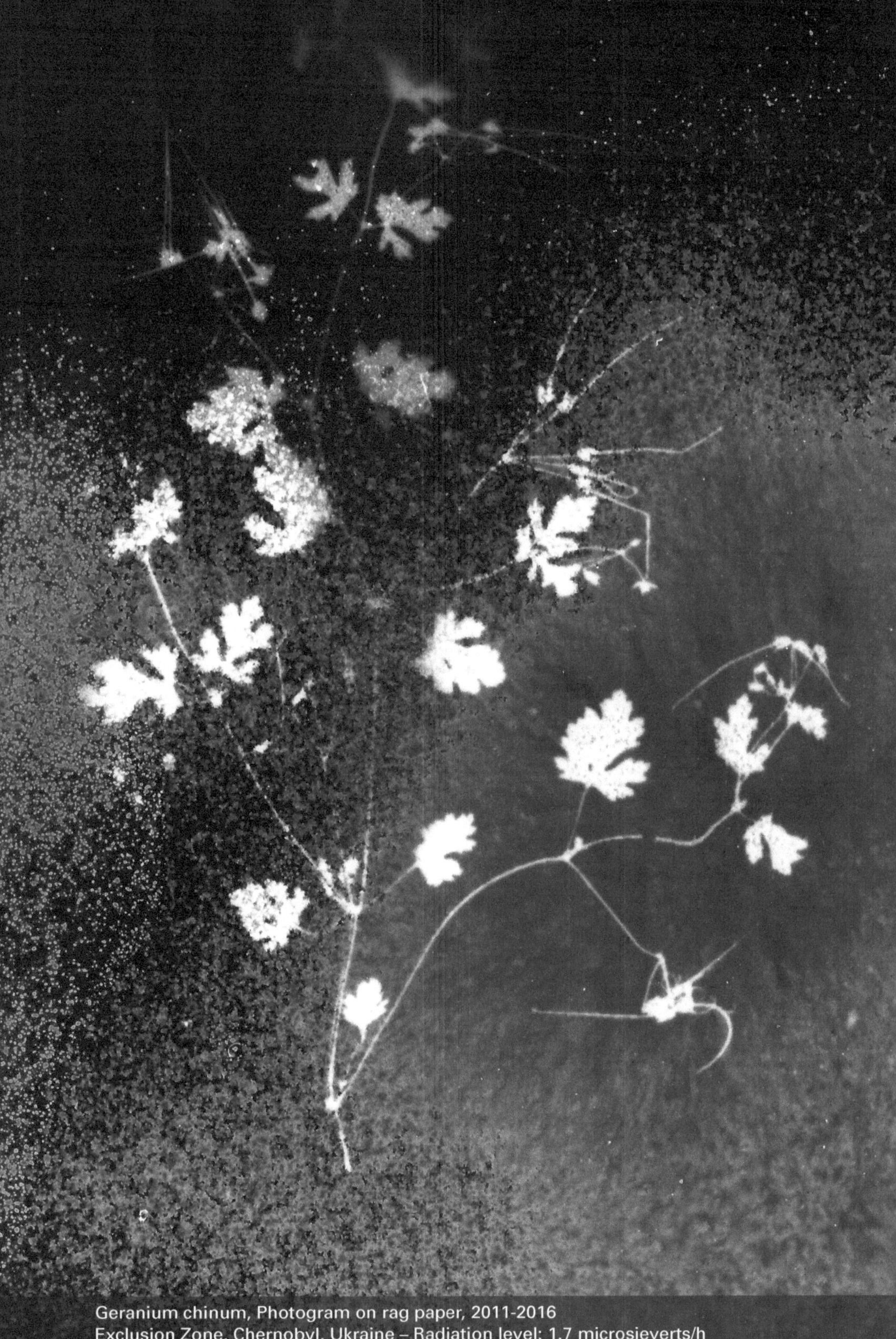

Geranium chinum, Photogram on rag paper, 2011-2016
Exclusion Zone, Chernobyl, Ukraine – Radiation level: 1.7 microsieverts/h

Fragment 6 **Exposure**

For over six weeks, from the end of April until mid-June 1986 I was exposed to massive quantities of radiation in Anapa. Most of that time was spent outdoors. At the beach. In the city's parks or promenades. Until not so long ago I was not aware of this, whether due to having undergone the uncanny non-experience at a young age or due to mistakenly believing that the plumes of radioactive materials travelled exclusively north, through Belorussia and the Baltic countries to Sweden and Norway, blazing new European cartographies.

It turns out, in retrospect, that I had exposure in common with animals and other humans, as well as with plants and the soil that received huge amounts of radiation without anyone being aware of it. I was, together with others in Anapa and further northwest in Kiev and Minsk, plant-like, or, to resort to an animal-based metaphor, "a sitting duck." What did our exposure amount to? Did it prepare the grounds for a trans-human solidarity? Its common denominator was physicality itself, the brute fact of having a physical extension, open to everything, including radiation. This openness spelled out unfathomable vulnerability, the incapacity to defend oneself from a threat that was unknown and undetectable by the sensorium. One is ineluctably passive in the face of radio*activity*.

We were all plants then. Except that vegetation is probably better at spotting radiation because it relentlessly receives, identifies, and processes the sun's ultraviolet rays, i.e., electromagnetic radiation all but invisible to us. Could it be that plants were more proficient in monitoring for ionizing radiation, as well? Rooted in the ground, they are of course unable to escape the harmful effects of radioactivity, as the pine trees in the so-called "red forest" close to the exclusion zone have attested. Yet, they are also more adaptable: soybeans experimentally grown in Chernobyl's radioactive environment have displayed drastic changes in their protein makeup, enabling them to improve their resistance to heavy metals and to modify their carbon metabolism.[5] Their exposure *to* the world is of one piece with learning *from* the world and giving plenty of things *back to* it. Only our, human, exposure betokens pure vulnerability, passivity, helplessness.

What about other kinds of exposure—for instance, that of photographs to light or of photograms to baths of chemicals that add unique visual effects? How many layers or levels of exposure are there before us? Who is the exposing and who or what the exposed? (I note *en passant* that the proliferation of words with the prefix *ex-* in these fragments—*ex*plosion, *ex*cess, *ex*posure, *ex*traordinary—is not accidental. I have, in fact, written an article about it.[6] Meaning *out* in Latin, this prefix conveys the movement of growth, pressing out, toward sunlight or deeper into the soil. In growing, the plant comes out of itself, is outside or beside itself twice over, already as a germinating seed. Vegetal life is not merely exposed; it *is* exposure, exteriority, outwardness. Only in limit circumstances can we *ex*perience on our very skin what vegetal being-exposed (or, generally speaking, being-*ex-*) implies. And, in still more rare situations, we realize in an *après coup* that we have been exposed without being cognizant of it at the time. We, the others of plants. But also, we, the other plants ...)

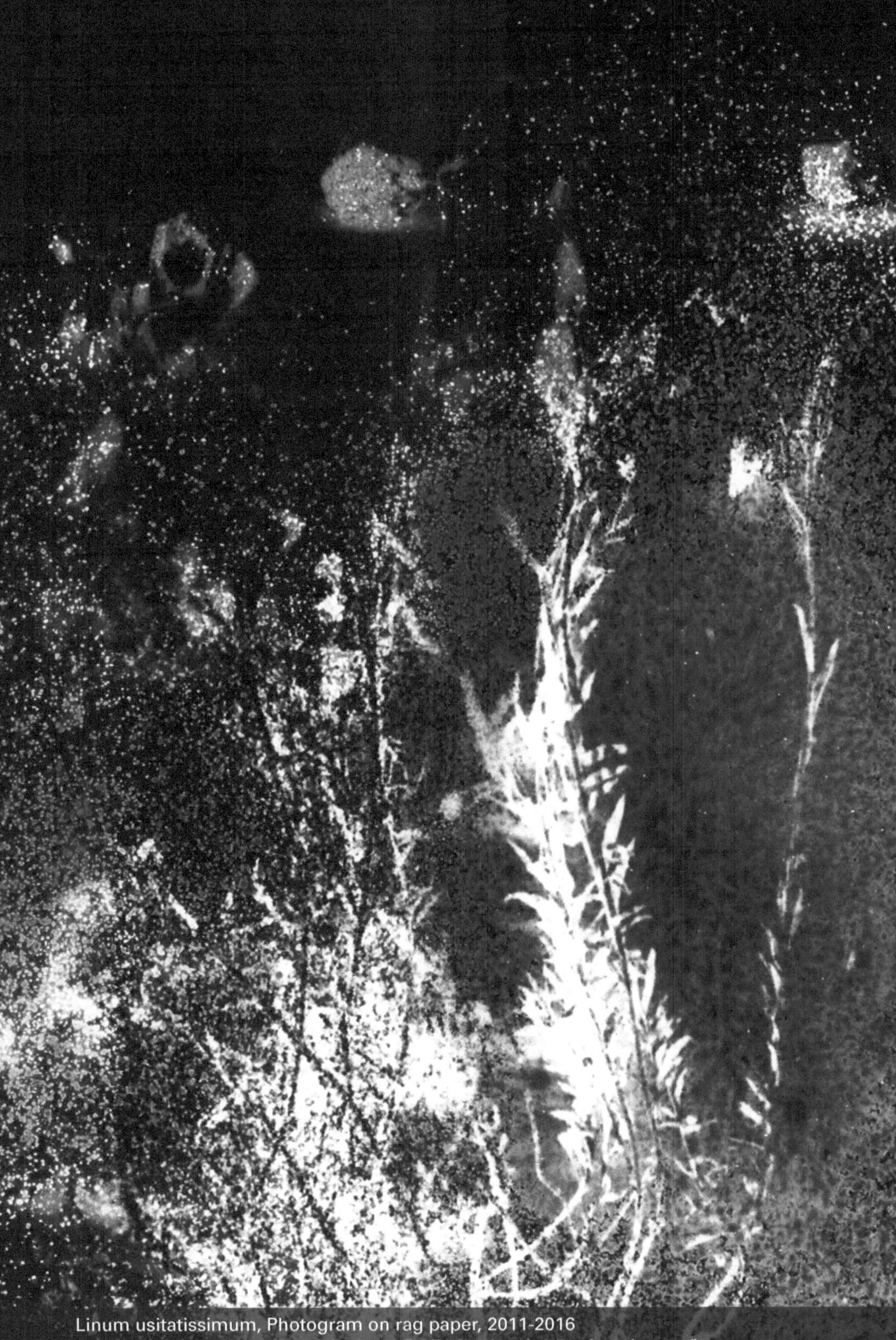

Linum usitatissimum, Photogram on rag paper, 2011-2016
Exclusion Zone, Chernobyl, Ukraine – Radiation level: 1.7 microsieverts/h

Fragment 7 **Silent witnessing**

It is incredibly difficult to talk and write about Chernobyl. No serious book on the subject has been able to dodge the task of thinking about the conditions of possibility for thinking in proximity to this theme or this scene. Still before commencing, a work on Chernobyl must first decide how to broach a theme that incessantly reverts back into the unthematizable.

As we have seen, the very structure of witnessing breaks down there where the event, with all its extraordinary, groundbreaking, and death-bearing potential, practically merges with everyday life thanks to its imperceptibility. What is there to say about exposure to radiation that cannot be seen nor smelled nor heard nor touched nor tasted? Those of us who have been in its eerie neighborhood have resembled objects, onto which certain effects have been inflicted, as opposed to subjects in control and aware of what is going on.

Bypassing our consciousness, material witnessing has been incorporated into us, becoming a part of the flesh: the radiation accumulated in the thyroid gland, the elements of strontium that, imitating calcium, have bound themselves to the bones ... Consciousness has been exploded not so much as an aftereffect of a violent shock but thanks to becoming superfluous. What is there to say, save for certifying the death of consciousness, which has outlived its usefulness when it comes to helping orient us in our environs in the wake of an unwieldy, unmanageable technology it, itself, had brought into being? All that remains is to perform an autopsy on it and to write its obituary, while envisioning, in the best of cases, the birth of another consciousness ...

Plants, too, live through occurrences without formulating them in speech. Their articulations are wholly material; the patterns observable on their extensions, from tree rings to the position of branches, are bodily witnesses to a history of growth and to its milieu. True: it is difficult to talk about Chernobyl. Then why not delegate testimonial acts to living beings that do not speak, at least not in human voices and languages, except if they are characters in sundry myths and fairytales? Why not assign such acts to plants? In some respects, Tondeur does just that. Were we to follow her artistic lead in thought, we would allow exposure to be translated into expression, and vulnerability—into a way of bearing witness.

Take a careful look at the pistils of this *Linum usitatissumum*. Aren't they both the radars, receiving stimulation from every side, receptive to pollen's secrets, and the loudspeakers, re-broadcasting wordless messages? Through the unique medium of photograms, Tondeur lets plants speak by spatially expressing themselves and the earth contaminated with radionuclides. Lines of light do not illuminate—from the external, neutral, and disengaged position of the third—the obscure traces of what happened. They bring out the testimony of the plant and of the soil wherein it grew.

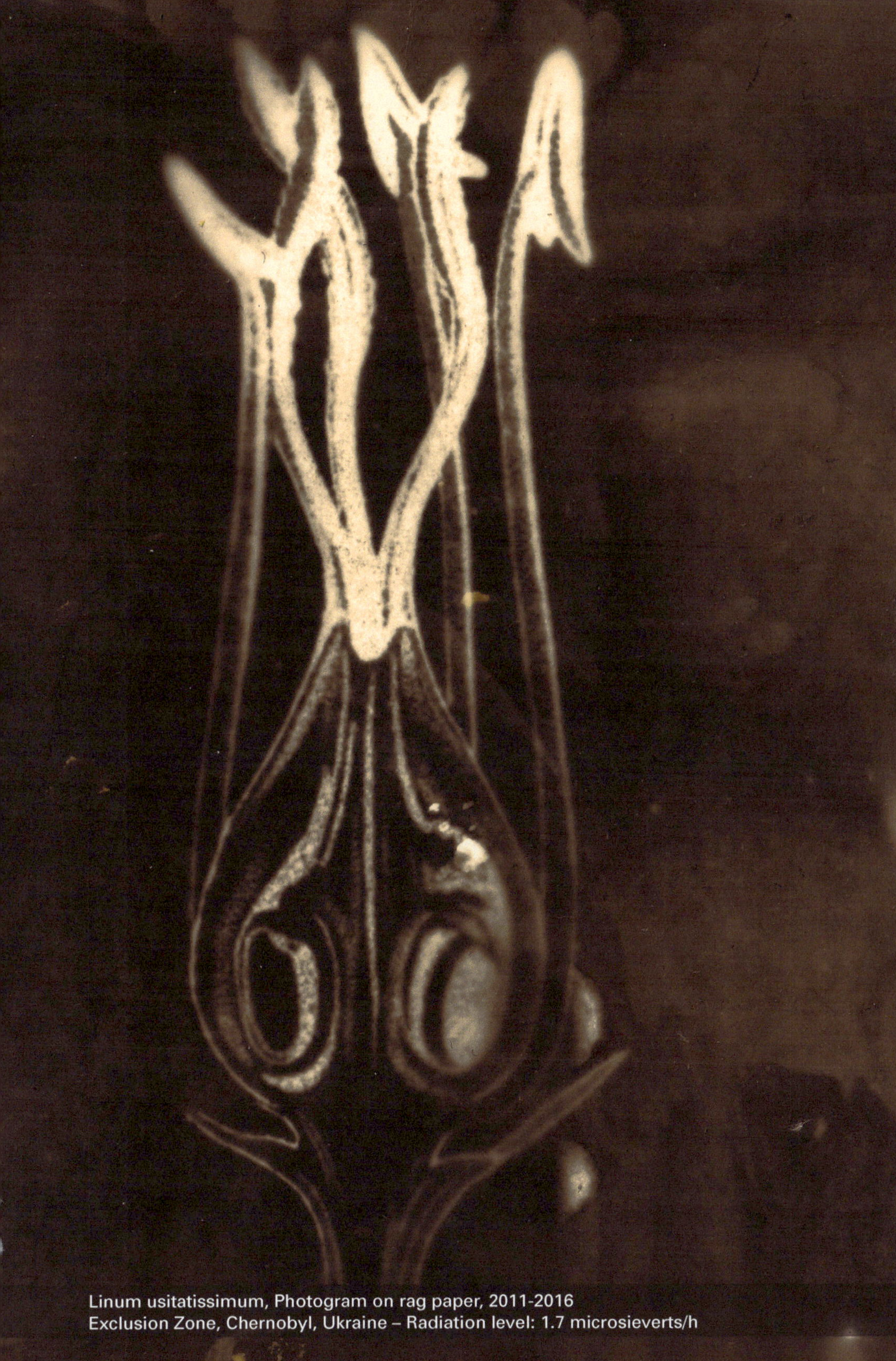

Linum usitatissimum, Photogram on rag paper, 2011-2016
Exclusion Zone, Chernobyl, Ukraine – Radiation level: 1.7 microsieverts/h

Fragment 8 **Energy nightmares**

Vegetal life is an excellent counterpoint to our default manner of producing energy, which culminated in Chernobyl. Plants process sunlight on their extended surfaces, the leaves. Their energy is, as I have noted in my previous work, essentially superficial, beholden to exteriority, and (with a few exceptions of the carnivorous varieties, incapable of photosynthesis) not destructive toward other entities. Plants receive everything they need to thrive from the elements: moisture and mineral nutrients in the soil and sunlight above the ground.

Animals and humans, on the other hand, procure energy otherwise, beginning with a distinct way of eating. They bite into whatever will nourish them, destroy its integrity, dig into the "energy reserve" into which the eaten is converted wholesale, and incorporate the nutrients and calories it contained into their own bodies. In obtaining energy, we break up and burn, reduce to basic components and extract, their valuable core from the objects of our needs and desires.

Remote as it may seem from these physiological processes, the quest for nuclear energy exacerbates their working principles, breaking down the seemingly indivisible (namely, the atom), and so peering into the deepest depths, the abyss of potency and potentiality. While conventional methods of "producing" energy had destroyed the formed matter of things, nuclear power devastated their very essence, the material principles that made them what they were.

Sublimated, and utterly sublime, digestion mutates. As the breakdown of matter is perfected, becoming more thorough and annihilating matter's very materiality, its byproducts turn virtually indigestible. Depleted radioactive materials are the new excrements of energy-hungry humankind, contaminating the environment for the time to come.

~

A recurrent dream: I float at sea, carried by the waves to another shore, that other shore where, towering high above, an exploded nuclear reactor is burning unabated, spewing raspberry-colored smoke into the air. Switching into nocturnal gear, where the past is distorted in keeping with fantasies and wish fulfillments, my psychic life embarks on a reverse journey to the source of radiation that had reached me in Anapa. And it amends geography along the way. Of course, the town of Pripyat', which serviced the Chernobyl nuclear power station, was situated on the banks of a river bearing the same name, not on the Black Sea. But dreams follow their own logic, simplifying or making reality more complex, as the case may be.

~

Building on the experience or the non-experience of Chernobyl, I'd like to propose that we not only cease using nuclear energy but also relinquish the paradigm that potentiated its use. I am referring here to the extractive-destructive attitude to the world, cast in terms of an energy container, its depths waiting to be breached, penetrated, and appropriated. The principal motivation behind my book, *Energy Dreams*, is to learn from plants how to live energetically having cured ourselves of our obsession with depth, to be devastated in the course of obtaining energy, and how to refrain from violence against others, human or not. At the same time, I am painfully aware of the fact that energy dreams have tended to morph into energy nightmares. For instance (and this is more than an example), the promise of cheap, efficient and "non-polluting" technologies that would offer abundant supplies of electricity has been associated with nuclear power. The fantasy of *perpetuum mobile*, presumably the antithesis of vegetal immobility, has mobilized existence as a whole, inching close to its annihilation.

We live in the shadow of an ever-present threat that our insatiable desire for energy would consume the entire world, without sparing us either. This threat is not an amorphous prospect. It has attained reality in April 1986, as well as, on scales of varying intensity, before and after that (Three Mile Island, Fukushima . . .). Still, the addiction to what is economically convenient is stronger than fear. Economy trumps ecology, albeit at the price of the environmental dwelling, the *oikos*, which we all inhabit and which inhabits us, which constitutes our very bodies. Heedless to the alarms that have been ringing for some time now, we have not yet woken up from our energy nightmares. If anything, they intensify, delineating the horizons of our present and, likely, of our future.

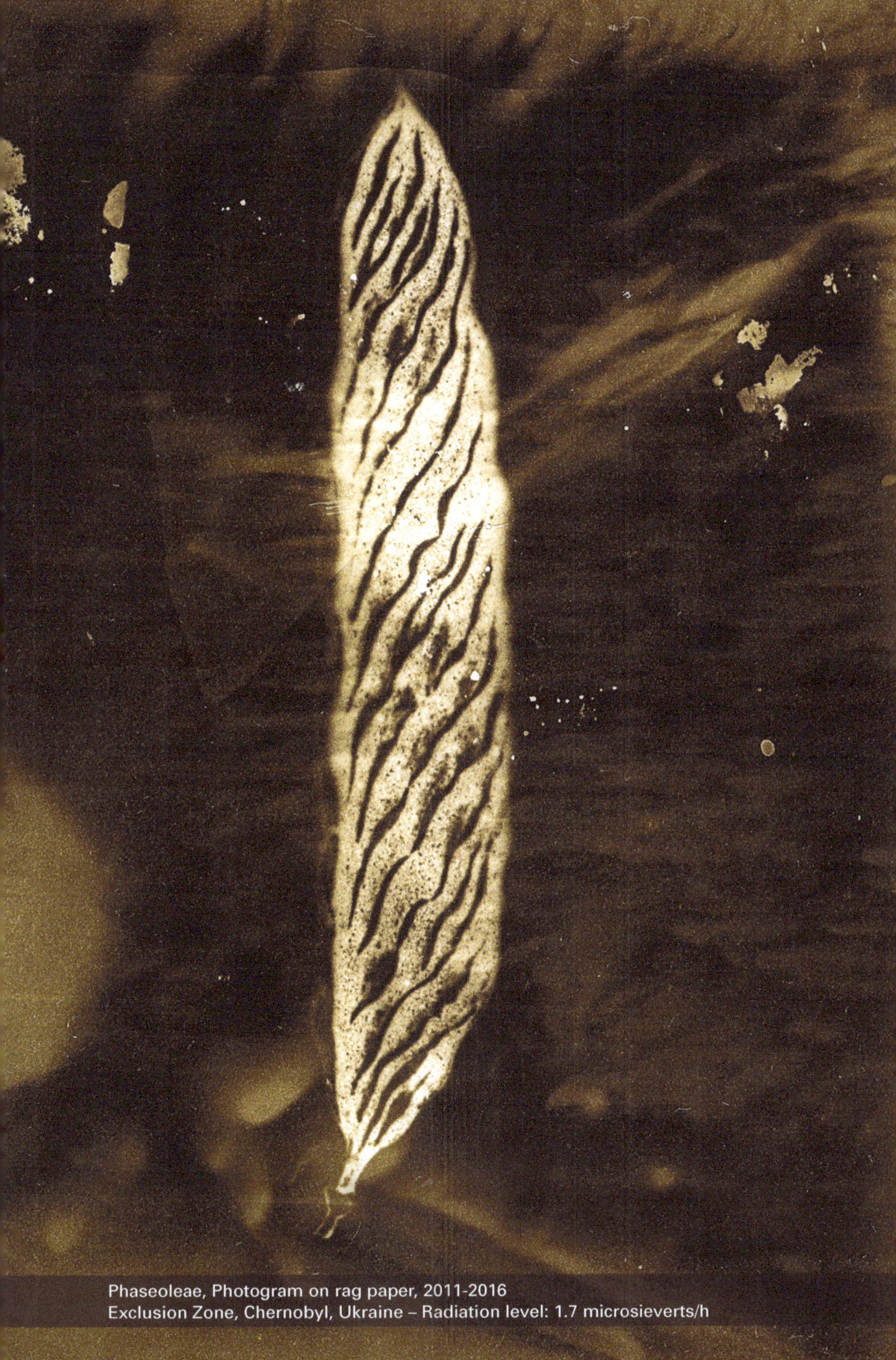

Phaseoleae, Photogram on rag paper, 2011-2016
Exclusion Zone, Chernobyl, Ukraine – Radiation level: 1.7 microsieverts/h

Fragment 9 **Fallen trees**

Visitors to the "red forest" near Chernobyl's ground zero observe the following scene. Here, pine trees turned reddish and perished shortly after the accident, their fallen trunks accumulating on the ground over the last thirty years. They are not decaying as they should,[7] nor being digested into the earth nor transformed into compost. The timescale of finite life has been disrupted and the same fate has befallen death as well, which is to say, the material afterlife of rotting and decay.

The fallen trees of the exclusion zone carry on the work of witnessing commenced by the living plants. They testify, among other things, to the impact of exorbitant radiation doses and of the technology that made their release possible on life, whose very loss is monumentalized in its external appearances, such as tree trunks and dry leaves, preserved as though they only fell yesterday. With the processes of decomposition stopped or slowed down as a result of damage done to the microbes, fungi, and insects responsible for the recycling of organic matter, it is as if life itself is stopped forever, frozen *and* irretrievably lost, notwithstanding recent reports of flora and fauna regeneration in the region.

Animals and plants are returning to Chernobyl's exclusion zone because human beings are gone, not because the soil is more fertile. We could celebrate this turn of events, finding in it a kind of laboratory for a vibrant planet that would survive the human onslaught long after our species is extinct. Or, we could fight against the nihilistic indifference, with which dead trees have been conserved (almost fossilized), through a concerted effort of selecting, arranging, and displaying traces of the catastrophe for the past and for the future, as a commemoration and a warning.

Now, to select, arrange, and display is to create a herbarium. Besides the plants that have grown in radioactive soil, the shards of our own exploded consciousness are reassembled in it, albeit not glued together—neither mended nor healed. In the fallen leaves and trees of Chernobyl, we can discern fragments of ourselves, of our bodies and thoughts. Having initially grown as plants do, they have become something other than vegetation, namely the ruins of our civilization, like the sarcophagus encasing the reactor mangled by the accident and like our pre-Chernobyl systems of thought shattered by what happened there.

A herbarium of injured plants, damaged bodies, and traumatized minds germinates, in all its dry glory, from the same malignant source as the disaster, which has no power over it, however. Picking up and caring for the rests, be they the products of vegetal or human activity, we try to give them their due, to rescue them from the waves of oblivion, to transfigure the deadly radioactive exposure they have endured into an aesthetic exposure of viewership, so that they would meet an empathetic, concerned, engaged, non-indifferent glance. Lifting whatever or whoever has fallen, this sublime herbarium singles out, raises, and elevates it, him, or her, even though such elevation is not tantamount to a resurrection. The lives that had too close of a brush with radiation's deadly invisible force have been lost forever. But they need not die a second time, to boot. That is, finally, what the work of mourning ensures: counteracting the twin urge to monumentalize the lost object or to consign it to absolute forgetting. "Successful" mourning permits the mourned representation to decay as it should, making space for future existence.

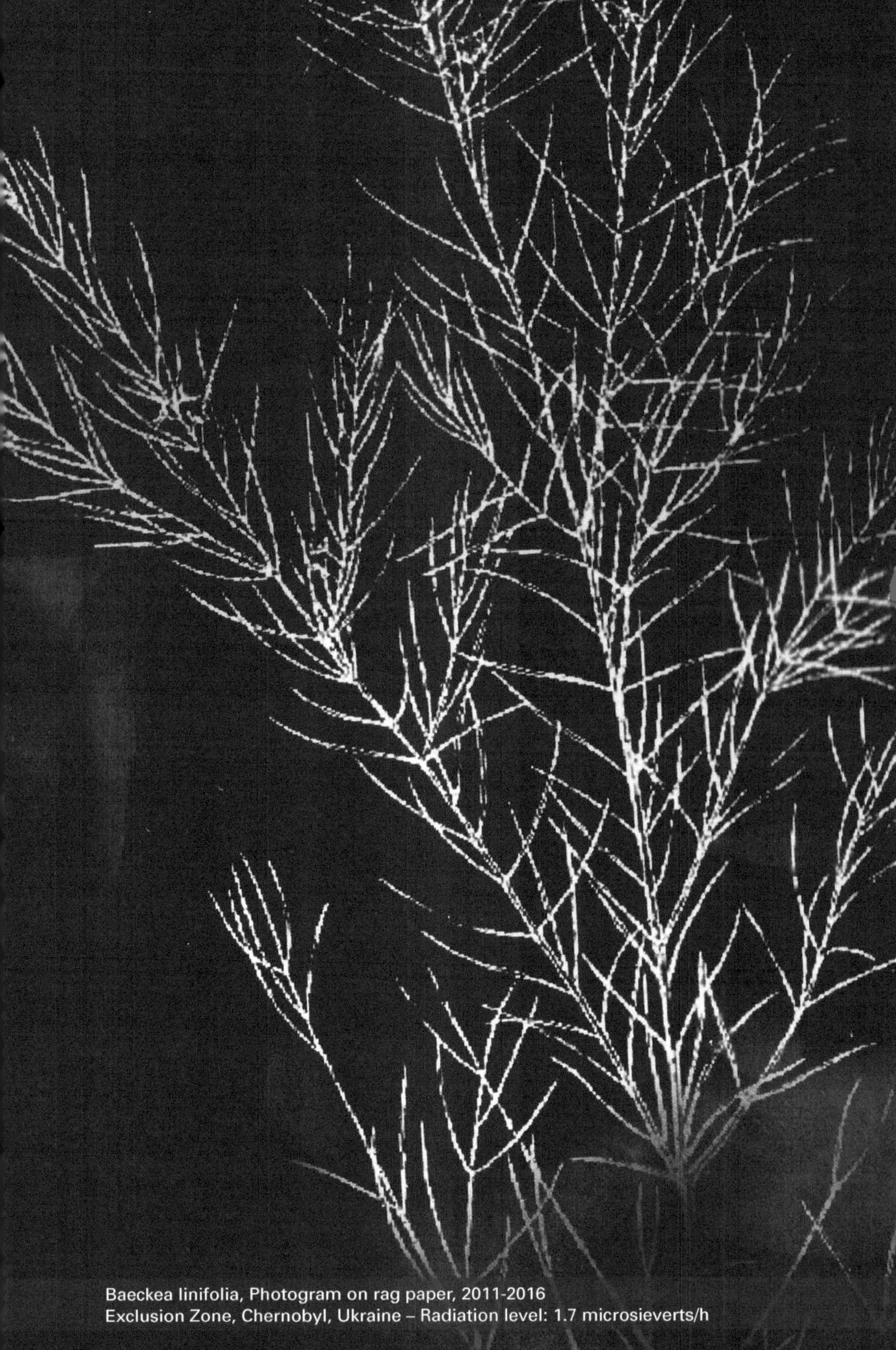

Baeckea linifolia, Photogram on rag paper, 2011-2016
Exclusion Zone, Chernobyl, Ukraine – Radiation level: 1.7 microsieverts/h

Fragment 10 **In Anapa**

The first thing I did, upon checking into a grey, hospital-like, government-run "sanatorium" (in Russian, this word does not designate a mental asylum but a place of rest and recovery for people afflicted by chronic illnesses), was rush to the beach so as to behold the vast expanse of water, extending as far as the eye could see. The experience was breathtaking.

From there, I walked with my father to a local bookstore, since I knew that the stash of books I had brought with me was bound to be depleted in the course of long reading sessions by the sea. I frequented the bookstore, within a ten-minute walking distance from our apartment in Moscow, almost daily. Luckily for me, it was located in the same building as the bakery, and I would make the inevitable detour to revisit books I had already leafed through and to look for fresh arrivals every time I was sent to buy bread. The Anapa store struck me with its paucity of choice, compared to the already limited selection I had been acquainted with in Moscow. Here, try as you would, you could find nothing other than the Soviet staples, like Nikolai Ostrovsky's *How Steel Was Tempered,* which was understandable given that even in the capital the classics of Russian literature, let alone books in translation, were "deficit items," available solely in exchange for coupons dispensed after you'd recycled tens of kilos of newspapers.

May 1 festivities were fast approaching and the city was ablaze with red flags and giant posters, proclaiming the virtues of the Communist path or consisting of the usual associations, such as "Peace, Labor, May." The main demonstration, similar to the selection of books, was much more modest than the manifestations I had participated in before. Exactly on that day, southeastern winds brought with them Chernobyl's radioactive fallout to Anapa. Needless to say, everything proceeded as scheduled; no changes to the program were made.

It was during these celebrations that an organizer of another festival caught up with me, asking if I was not, by any chance, a Georgian child from a Soviet republic situated about 200 kilometers south of Anapa. Undeterred by a negative response, she suggested that I would be a perfect fit for the role she envisioned. Dressed in a traditional costume, I would represent Georgia at a carnival of Soviet multiculturalism, slated to take place on my birthday, two days after the May 1 festivities. I agreed and was immediately issued an ankle long woolen Chokha (a typical outfit worn by men from the Caucasus Mountains), replete with the widest belt I'd ever seen, a fake sabre and an extra-warm headpiece. That is how I appeared and danced at the festival, when radiation levels in the atmosphere peaked, finding my outfit unbearably hot but probably receiving minimal radiation protection from it.

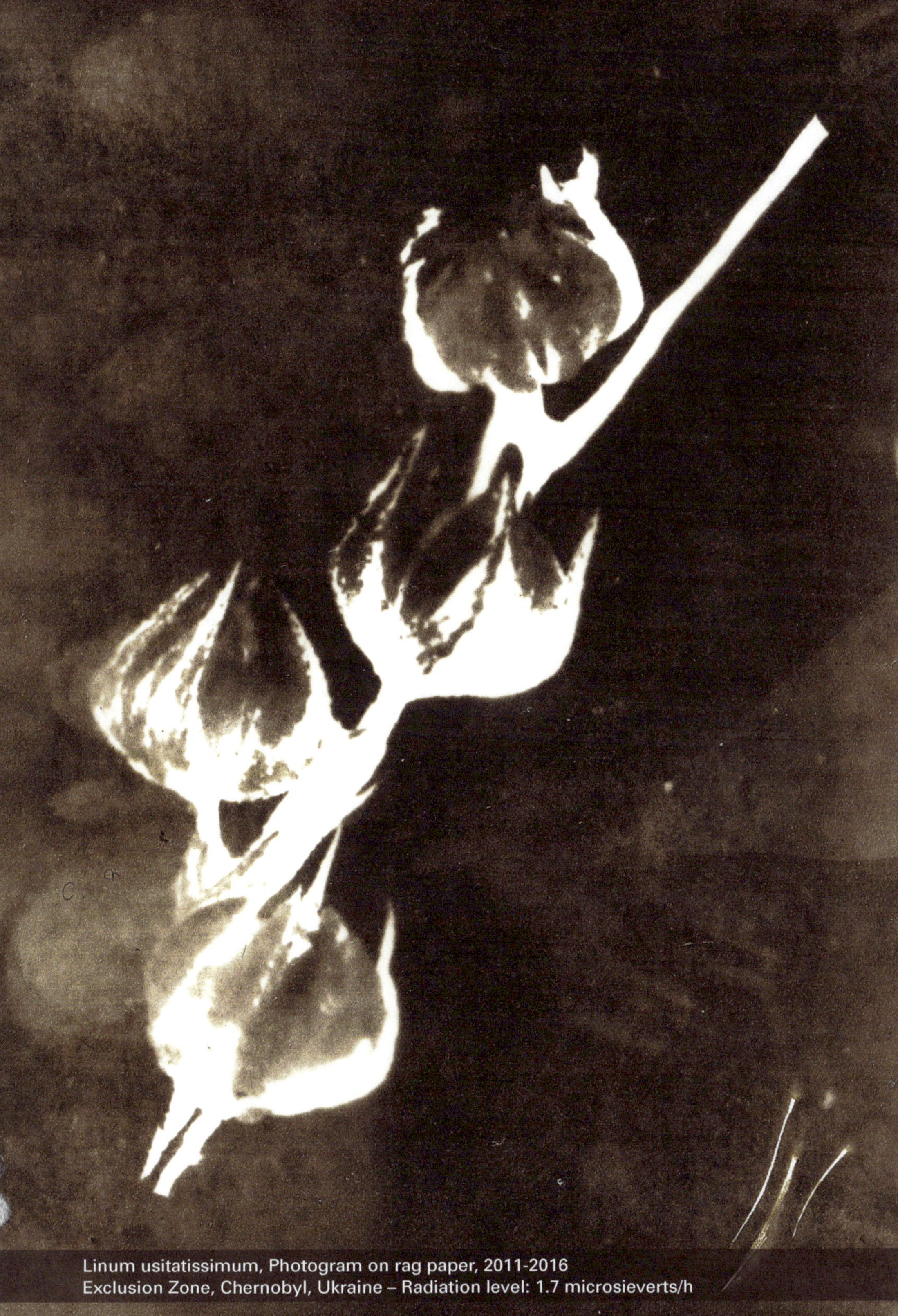

Linum usitatissimum, Photogram on rag paper, 2011-2016
Exclusion Zone, Chernobyl, Ukraine – Radiation level: 1.7 microsieverts/h

Fragment 11 **From shadows on a wall to imprints on a sheet**

At the very end of October 2015, Inês Cardoso, who curates contemporary art in London, drew my attention to the works of Anaïs Tondeur, gathered under the heading *At the Edge of the Visible*. Inês thought—and rightly so!—that I would be keenly interested in the plants that comprised Tondeur's photogrammic studies of specimens grown in Chernobyl's exclusion zone.

By pure chance, this indication came at a time when I was reading Alexievich's *Voices from Chernobyl*, recalling and reflecting upon my own eerie proximity to the abyss denoted by that name. The encounter with Tondeur's artworks felt like a piece of a puzzle that fell into its proper spot, extending a bridge between my theoretical concerns with plant life, with the philosophy behind energy production, and certain autobiographical preoccupations. Within a few days, Anaïs and I started planning the book you are reading at this very moment as an artistic-philosophical collaboration.

In our subsequent exchange, Anaïs intimated that, at a symbolic level, she resorted to the technique of photograms with the view to leading our imagination back to the shadows cast by people or objects on the walls of Hiroshima and Nagasaki after the atomic bombings of these Japanese cities in August 1945. That, to me, sounded like an evocative and powerful way of establishing interconnections between humans and plants, cementing the trans-species and trans-kingdoms solidarity of victims, and unearthing the co-imbrication of the "peaceful" and "military" uses of nuclear technologies. The radiation released from the two atomic bombs that had been dropped on Hiroshima and Nagasaki transformed city surfaces, if not the entire world, into so many screens, onto which living photograms were emblazoned.

The photosensitive paper that came into contact with plants from the exclusion zone recalled these urban imprints and the meltdown of Chernobyl's Reactor 4 forty-one years after the American nuclear bombing of Japan. Still, we cannot overlook a key difference between the shadows on the wall and the Chernobyl Herbarium. There is no aesthetics of war, suffering, and death—only their *post factum* aestheticization. The existence that has been fragmented and cut short can and does turn up in literary texts and works of art: say, in Pablo Picasso's *Guernica* or Maurice Blanchot's narrative "The Instant of My Death," discussed by Jacques Derrida.[8] Even so, the most horrifying and moving aesthetic productions are not war, suffering, and death *themselves* but reminiscences that, as I have written above, signify "release and preservation; preservation and release: by the grace of art."

Vegetal imprints on photosensitive surfaces do not repeat the violence of Hiroshima, Nagasaki, and Chernobyl. They resonate with mute suffering and give it a chance to speak, without resorting to voices and words (whispered or screamed out), without adding or subtracting images and representations, without as much as depicting violence *qua* violence, which was not sensed in the open, as an object of experience, by anyone who was not in the immediate vicinity of the exploded nuclear reactor. Amazingly, regardless of their multiple associations with the realized nuclear threat, Tondeur's photograms channel nothing but beauty. Analogous to the Buddhist meditation practice of Tonglen ("Giving and Receiving"), they breathe suffering into the aesthetic medium and exhale comfort, compassion, and peace.

And what of time's relentless passage? We would be lucky were we to linger on as shadows on a wall or imprints on a sheet after it's done with its work.

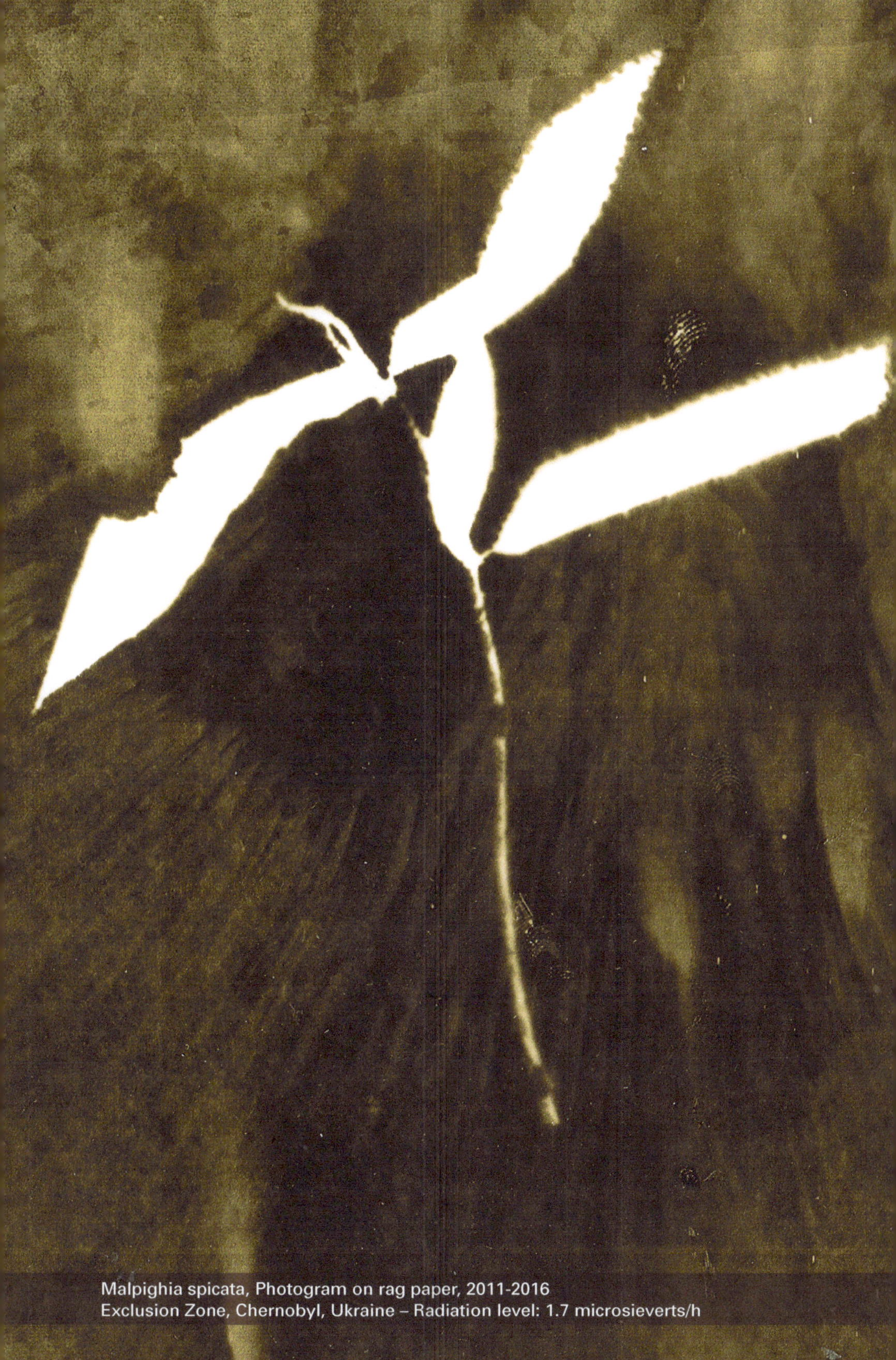

Malpighia spicata, Photogram on rag paper, 2011-2016
Exclusion Zone, Chernobyl, Ukraine – Radiation level: 1.7 microsieverts/h

Fragment 12 **Risk**

We've heard the stories of first responders, also known as *the liquidators,* to the Chernobyl fallout—people who, unequipped with protective gear, combatted the fire that broke out after a series of blasts in Reactor 4 and those who, later on, participated in the decontamination effort, for instance, by removing layers of radioactive soil and burying it deeper in the earth. Their numbers reaching 200,000, the liquidators developed chronic illnesses and died as a consequence of radiation poisoning. Honored as heroes, often postmortem, many among them willingly risked their lives by acting for the sake of others and not caring about themselves. They behaved in accord with the official Soviet ideology of selflessness, altruism, and the value of the collective over the individual, the ideology they had internalized and avowed as their own.

On the face of it, the romanticizing of risk is diametrically opposed to the Western emphasis on safety, security, and risk-avoidance, but this opposition is largely mistaken. Lurking behind the discourses of personal, alimentary, and energy security is not the cancellation but a tacit displacement of risk, its global reallocation to those most vulnerable. Ulrich Beck hinted at this predicament in his groundbreaking studies, published precisely in the decade of the Chernobyl tragedy.[9]

Today, risk is a sort of negative ontological capital that expands alongside industrial or postindustrial (financial) capital and is passed on to the very populations that are dispossessed of material wealth and prosperity. As such, it is subject to calculation, assessment, and privatization, which was all the rage after the Fukushima meltdown, when health risks, the hazards pertaining to environmental "externalities," and the economic costs of tackling the consequences of nuclear contamination were transferred from TEPCO and the Japanese government to the citizens.[10]

The calculus of probabilities and risk management are the privilege of the few who feel safe at present and who wish to maintain the status quo, afraid that their safety would be compromised in the future. They are little consolation to the people, animals, plants, and ecosystems who or that find themselves on the losing side of the algorithms and the equations. More than that, with regard to nuclear accidents and climate change alike, risk management is futile because the environment, which could be made unlivable in an instant or over a more protracted period, is shared by all humans and by all non-human species. Confronted with these threats to the elemental commons, we are (or should be) communists, if only we think a little outside the frame of mindless, mechanical calculations and property considerations. Global "food and energy security," too, is a gateway to a more troubling insecurity, associated with eroding soils, increased CO2 emissions, and the loss of biodiversity. Such discourses ignore the risks faced by plants and animals, rivers, forests, and the earth, especially insofar as these exceed "our" environment and deserve moral consideration in and of themselves.

~

Thirty years subsequent to what happened in Chernobyl, the risks of using atomic energy are no longer a matter of the future; they are the already actualized threats that spill over into and overshadow the present. The greatest risk, not amenable to any calculative machinations, is carrying on as though the 1986 explosion did not rock the power station, built on the banks of Pripyat', along with our consciousness. As though the world and our picture of it were still intact. As though the self-regenerative capacities of the body and of the environment were endless. As though finitude were infinitely resilient, ready to be reborn from the ashes each time anew, like the Phoenix we mistake it for.

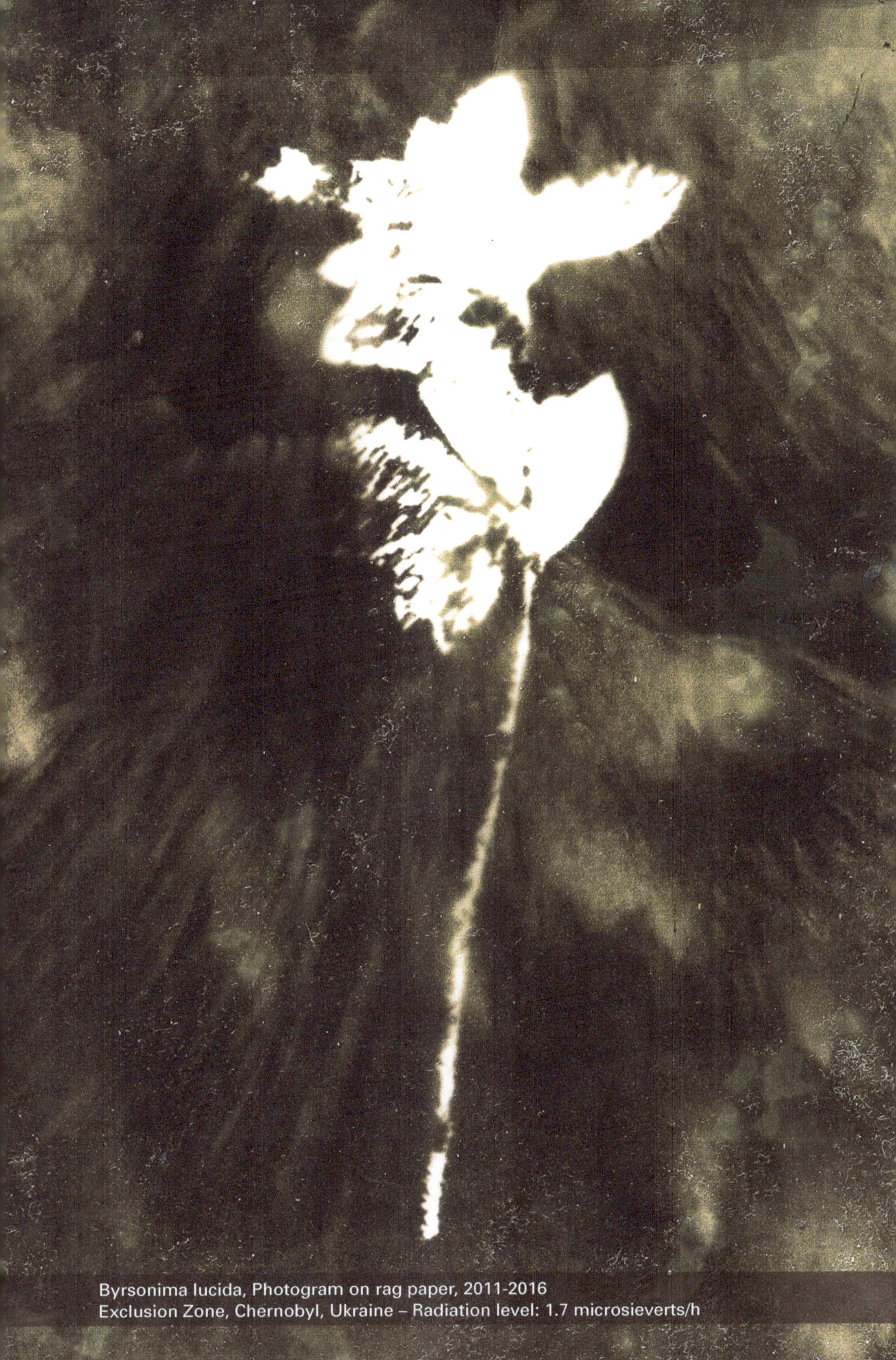

Byrsonima lucida, Photogram on rag paper, 2011-2016
Exclusion Zone, Chernobyl, Ukraine – Radiation level: 1.7 microsieverts/h

Fragment 13 **What is a herbarium?**

Less than two years ago, I published a book, *The Philosopher's Plant: An Intellectual Herbarium,*[11] where I invited readers for a stroll through Western philosophy's gardens, fields, and forests. I sought help from vegetal metaphors and allegories, processes and phenomena, which I then associated with the intellectual achievements of twelve thinkers, from Greek Antiquity to our days. While Mathilde Roussel made fantastic drawings, imagining plant-human hybrids, I noted by way of introduction that a herbarium is far from "a monumental contribution" shedding light on "deep conceptual connections." It is traversed, rather, by a group of "family resemblances" among plants and/or among thinkers.[12] My aim was to undermine the smooth and translucent narrative of Western metaphysics, with its insistence on the unity and stability of thought, and to replay its history of aspirations to the immutable through a procession of inherently changeable beings, the metamorphosing plants.

Encountering Tondeur's Chernobyl series, I instantaneously got an inkling of what I had to accomplish. Having compiled a herbarium of philosophical systems, I can try to assemble a *hortus siccus* of shattered, shaken, damaged lives, vegetal and human, including my own. Like the plants it houses, a herbarium is essentially superficial, accentuating, for the most part, the shapes and colors of dry specimens, that is, surfaces refracting light. An avid botanist and collector of herbaria, Jean-Jacques Rousseau saw in the collections of conserved plants prescient indications regarding the simplicity and refreshing superficiality of vegetal life. So much so that he defined botany as the best science, most closely allied with nature and naturalness, against chemistry,[13] which dissolved the forms of things into compounds and molecules, eating into matter and probing depth at the price of appearance.

That said, Tondeur's Chernobyl Herbarium does not correspond to Rousseau's specifications. For one, it does not feature the plants themselves but their impressions on a photosensitive surface. For another, it is mediated by chemicals, in which the paper retaining their imprints is bathed. Mind you, these modifications are quite telling. They imply that there is no more untouched simplicity of nature, no more unspoiled beauty after Chernobyl, no safety valves or escape routes from civilization, least of all in our bodies or in the corporeality of plants.

We should not succumb to profound pessimism or nihilism, though. The Chernobyl Herbarium is still a surface-to-surface encounter of vegetation with photosensitive paper. And it still contains something of the curative force I have, a little hurriedly, identified as "the grace of art," the force Rousseau deemed to be "his unique '*pharmacie*',"[14] into which he could tap through his study of botany and the creation of herbaria. This force is powerless to effect a change in reality, to penetrate its core and decontaminate the bodies of the earth, of animals, plants and humans laced with radioactive isotopes. But, precisely, its powerlessness and desistence from depth are its virtues. It strokes the surfaces of things—the superficies of the remains, including the fragments of the thing called *psyche*—consoling them, patting them, offering gentle contact, caress. It is possible to be touched without a modicum of sentimentality. When I chanced upon the photograms, I was touched in this very sense, attaining a different level of self-knowledge thanks to them. (A full stop and final period for now, because we are already sliding into the singular.)

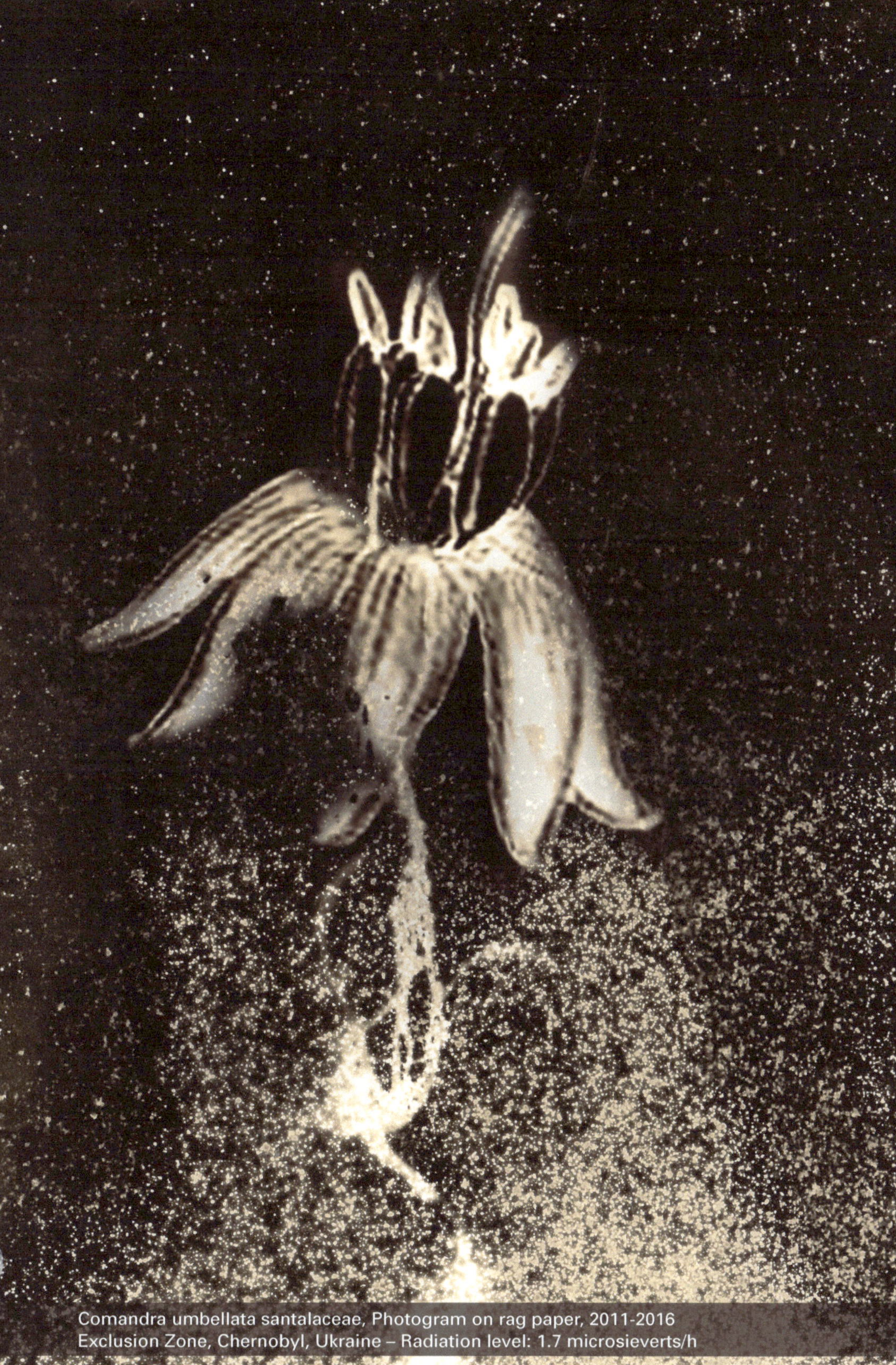

Comandra umbellata santalaceae, Photogram on rag paper, 2011-2016
Exclusion Zone, Chernobyl, Ukraine – Radiation level: 1.7 microsieverts/h

Fragment 14 **Radiation's countless afterlives**

The half-life of depleted uranium (U-238) is the same as the age of our planet: 4.5 billion years, a time span that, compared to the entire human history, is virtually infinite. Cesium-137 is more unassuming. It has a half-life of three decades, which means that by the thirtieth anniversary of "Chernobyl" (the name of the site as the metonymy for what happened there) only fifty percent of cesium-137 atoms that have been discharged into the environment will have been transformed into barium-137 with a half-life of about 2.5 minutes. A similar ratio is applicable to strontium-90, with a half-life of 28 years.

Radiation has multiple afterlives, conventionally measured by the period it takes for half the radioactive atoms to be transformed into more stable elements. The residual atoms will be equally divided between those that will require the same amount of time to undergo a transformation and those that will keep their radioactivity until the next cycle halves them. And so on... Because certain isotopes exhibit chemical similarities to the constituents of our bodies, they can be incorporated into us. Strontium-90, akin to calcium, becomes a part of the bone structure. It is taken up into our skeletons, our teeth... Subsequent to the start of worldwide nuclear weapons testing, this isotope is present in the dental makeup of anyone born after 1963. The peregrinations of radioactive materials continue in us, as us. Chernobyl's human survivors are the scraps of radiation's afterlife, which severely limits life expectancy as a consequence of external and, in many cases, ongoing internal exposures. Plants grown in contaminated soil are, likewise, a finite afterlife of radiation. Strontium-90 accumulates in vascular vegetal tissues, whereas cesium-137 is distributed throughout a plant, due to its similarity to potassium.[15]

But then there is art.

If the plants of Chernobyl are an afterlife of radiation, then Tondeur's photograms are the afterlife of that afterlife, a variation on the theme "the copy of a copy" that, since Plato, has determined the outlines of the aesthetic domain. The imprints portend survival, the afterglow of what gives itself to sight. They reflect the lived, and outlived, meaning. In contrast to the Platonic hierarchy, with the unproduced and originary Ideas at its apex followed by a descending chain of increasingly pale reproductions, the photograms faithfully accompany the "horizontal" metamorphoses of life, as much as the countless afterlives of formed matter, light, radiation... Outside the purview of metaphysical philosophy that treats it as a collection of simulacra, art respects time, or, perhaps, it rebels *against time within time*, serving as a paradoxical, non-dialectical medium for preservation-and-release. Art today is nothing, if not an emblem—being thrown into, *emballein*—of afterlife.

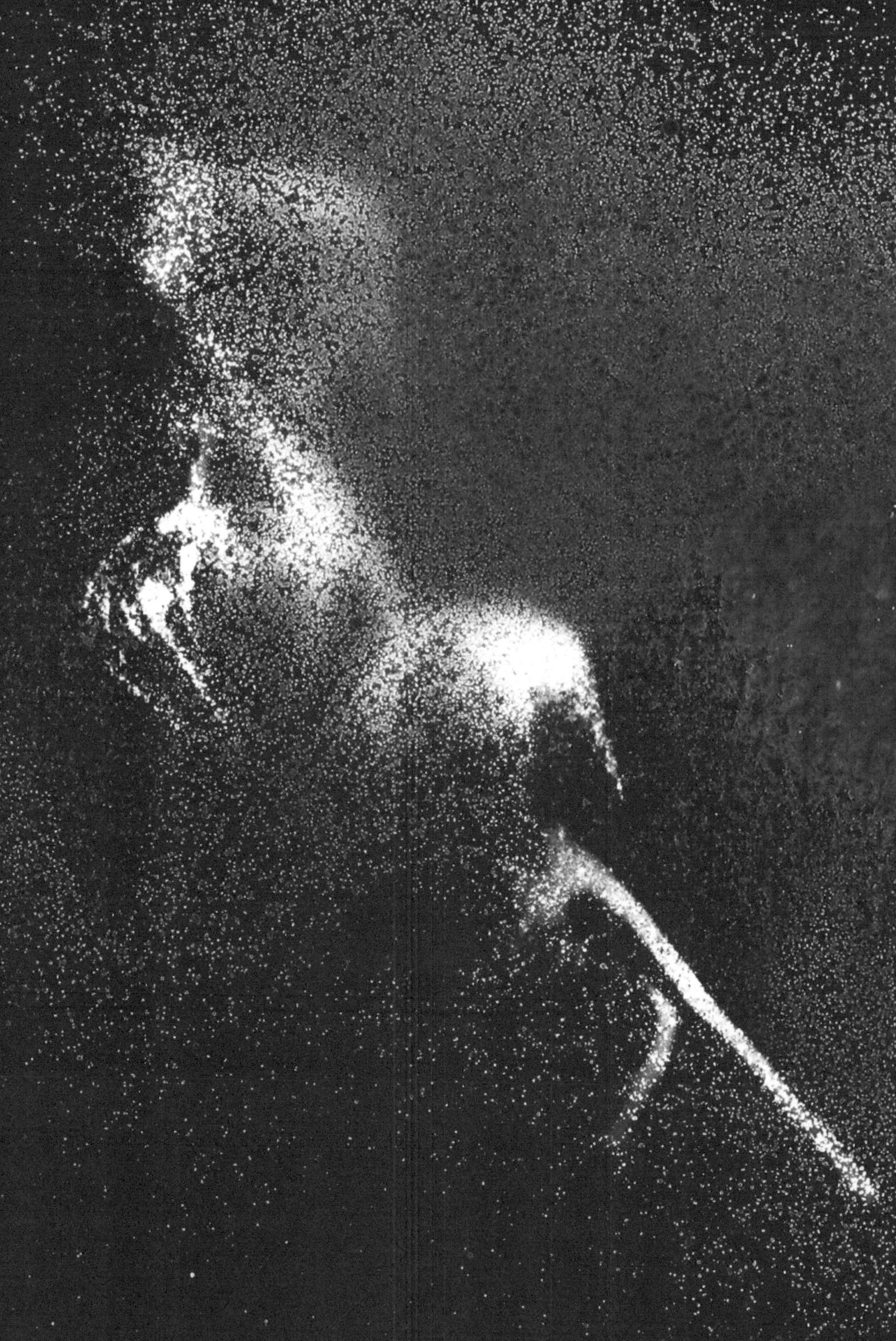

Linum usitatissimum, Photogram on rag paper, 2011-2016
Exclusion Zone, Chernobyl, Ukraine – Radiation level: 1.7 microsieverts/h

Fragment 15 **The system implodes**

Much has been said about the historical knot that tied Chernobyl together with Soviet Union's collapse. For all the inebriating freedom people felt when Gorbachev instituted his reforms, inaugurating *perestroika* (which translates as "rebuilding") and *glasnost'* ("vociferousness"), they were denied access to vital information with tremendous impact on their health and the state of the environment. The values of *perestroika* and *glasnost'* were readily discarded at a time of crisis, a decision that would continue to haunt the Soviet leadership until the regime's final days. Reactor 4 at Chernobyl's nuclear power station, suggestively named after V.I. Lenin, exploded; the political and economic system that had constructed it imploded under the weight of its bureaucracy, inner contradictions, ideological exhaustion, and the unwinnable competition with the "capitalist West."

As for the shattering of the Soviet consciousness, it was both an explosion and an implosion, not as sudden as the former and not as gradual as the latter. A vast majority of those who lived through it took cognizance of what had transpired only after the event, in a way strikingly analogous to how the complex of occurrences that goes under the name "Chernobyl" was existentially interpreted, *après coup*. (Typical anecdotal reports repeat ad nauseam: "One fine morning, I woke up and, although everything seemed the same as before, I no longer recognized my country." To this day, many dismiss this rude awakening as part of a nightmare, a horrible dream. Their denial is at the root of contemporary Russian politics.)

I was deeply affected (at the time, unawares) by the Chernobyl explosion and by the Soviet implosion. My body and mind took in the effects of both. A little over a year after the trip to Anapa, I entered the first grade at an elementary school where teachers could, for the first time in decades, use experimental pedagogic methods and draft their own class curricula. I appreciate that, in my formative years, I benefited from a newly found openness, inventiveness, and autonomy in teaching—attitudes that, in one way or another, still influence my scholarly pursuits. But given that the "foundations" I rely upon include an explosion and an implosion, my existence is vertiginously groundless (that is to say: intensely *existential*, a true throw), a predicament exacerbated by an acute sense of non-belonging and a series of subsequent displacements. The collapse of the Soviet Union enabled my first immigration. The event (or the non-event) of Chernobyl added to my disquiet. Extremes intersected: the implosion led to exile; the explosion instigated further introspection.

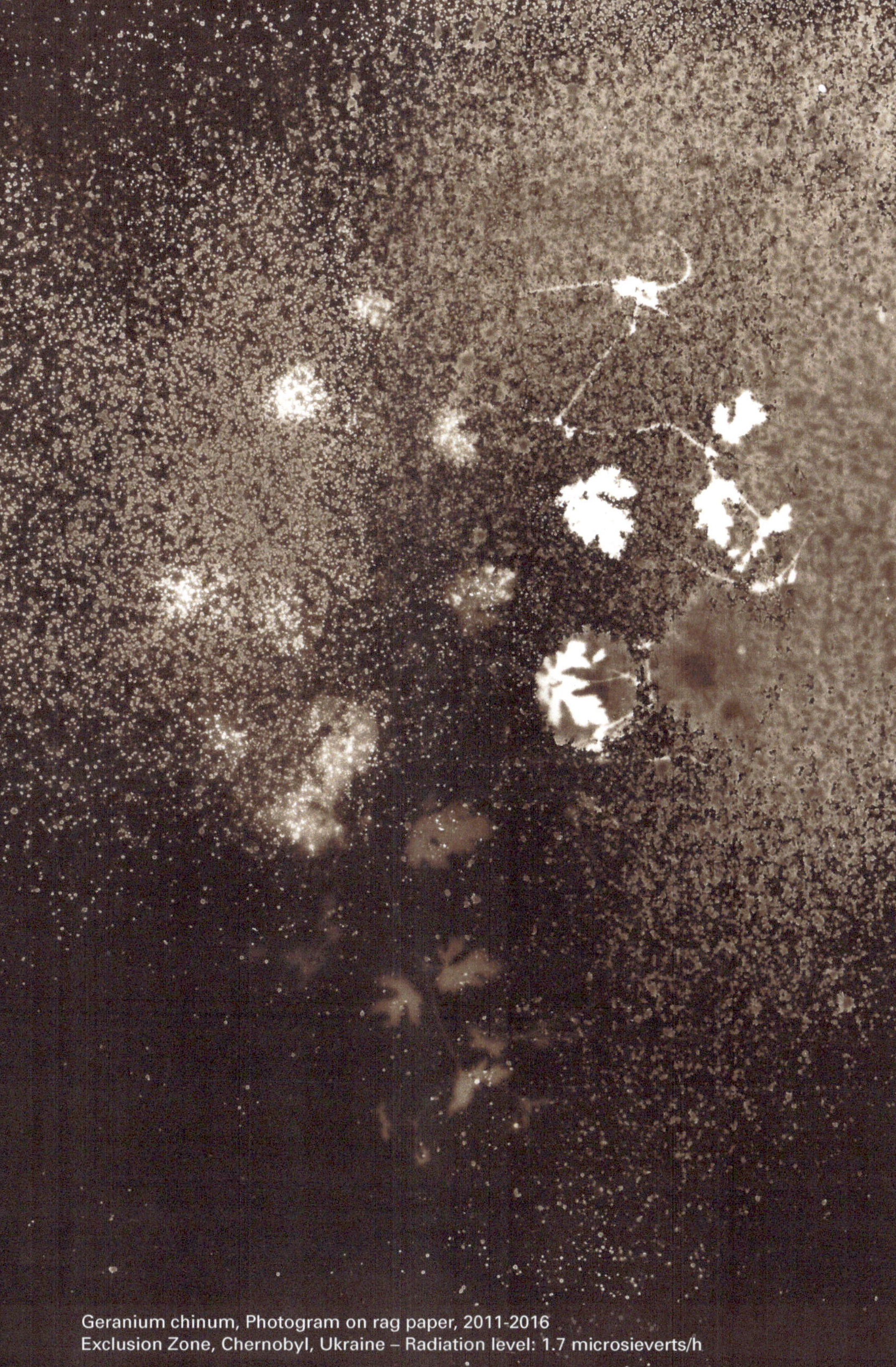

Geranium chinum, Photogram on rag paper, 2011-2016
Exclusion Zone, Chernobyl, Ukraine – Radiation level: 1.7 microsieverts/h

Fragment 16 **Chernobyl, the place and the word**

Following a brief delay due to the Soviet cover-up, Chernobyl has—overnight and the world over—morphed into a symbol of tragedy, a disaster all the more fearsome because of its imperceptible and yet inscrutable effects. It has evoked everything from the chimeras of genetic mutations to "glowing" plants, animals, and humans. And, regardless of the time that has passed, it still functions as a cipher for an unmarked trauma, a *shibboleth* for the irremediable dearth of understanding, a barbed-wire limit to interpretation, which does not allow us to draw on past experience so as to imbue the arcane disaster with meaning.

Prior to the night of April 26, 1986, Chernobyl was just a small town in northern Ukraine, situated less than two hundred kilometers from Berdychiv, where my maternal grandfather hailed from. Like other settlements in the area (Jitomir and Vinnitsa stand out for me, because some of my more distant relatives come from there), it was home to significant numbers of Ashkenazi Jews, who accounted for sixty percent of its inhabitants at the turn of the twentieth century. Since the end of the eighteenth century, Chernobyl was the center of an important Hasidic dynasty founded by an itinerant preacher Nahum.[16]

On a darker side, and similar to other neighboring towns (or, in Yiddish, the *shtetls*), it was the site of horrific pogroms that decimated the Jewish population. During the civil war, many of Chernobyl's Jews were burnt alive by the Cossacks in a local synagogue.[17] Under the German occupation that began in 1941, the surviving Jewish residents of Chernobyl were shot *en masse* right at the cemetery, where their ancestors were buried and where, on the site of their collective grave, a nondescript tombstone commemorating the atrocities was erected after the war. Symbolically, therefore, Chernobyl names a catastrophe before catastrophe, the one overlaying and overwriting the other. That "other Chernobyl" is, to this day, hidden, buried, forgotten, now also under piles of radioactive debris.

The literal meaning of the word itself sends us back to plants: *chyornyi byllia* is "black grass," or mugwort, the botanical species *Artemisia vulgaris*. Dedicated to the Greek goddess Artemis, it was supposed to be a plant that imparted strength and endurance, offered protection, and facilitated healing. The magical powers of *Artemisia vulgaris* have, alas, floundered and heartbreak upon heartbreak, bodymindbreak upon bodymindbreak, are unhealed! The Chernobyl disaster is a mugwort disaster—not, to be sure, of the mugwort itself, but of our relation to it and, through it, to vegetal nature as, at once, a part and a condensed representation of nature as a whole.

What exploded in Chernobyl was more than a nuclear reactor. Its ultimate casualty was the future of human dwelling in what we succinctly term our *natural environment*: in the midst of the elements of air and water, the earth and solar fire; with plants and animals; in proximity to forests and rivers, such as Pripyat'. It was symptomatic of the loss of a world where one could still breathe, live, and just be, the loss which could be sudden, triggered by an explosion, or gradual as in the case of global climate change. If practical consciousness lets us move quite effortlessly in our physical milieu, then the collapse of our immediate environment necessarily results in the detonation of consciousness. That is when thinking really begins.

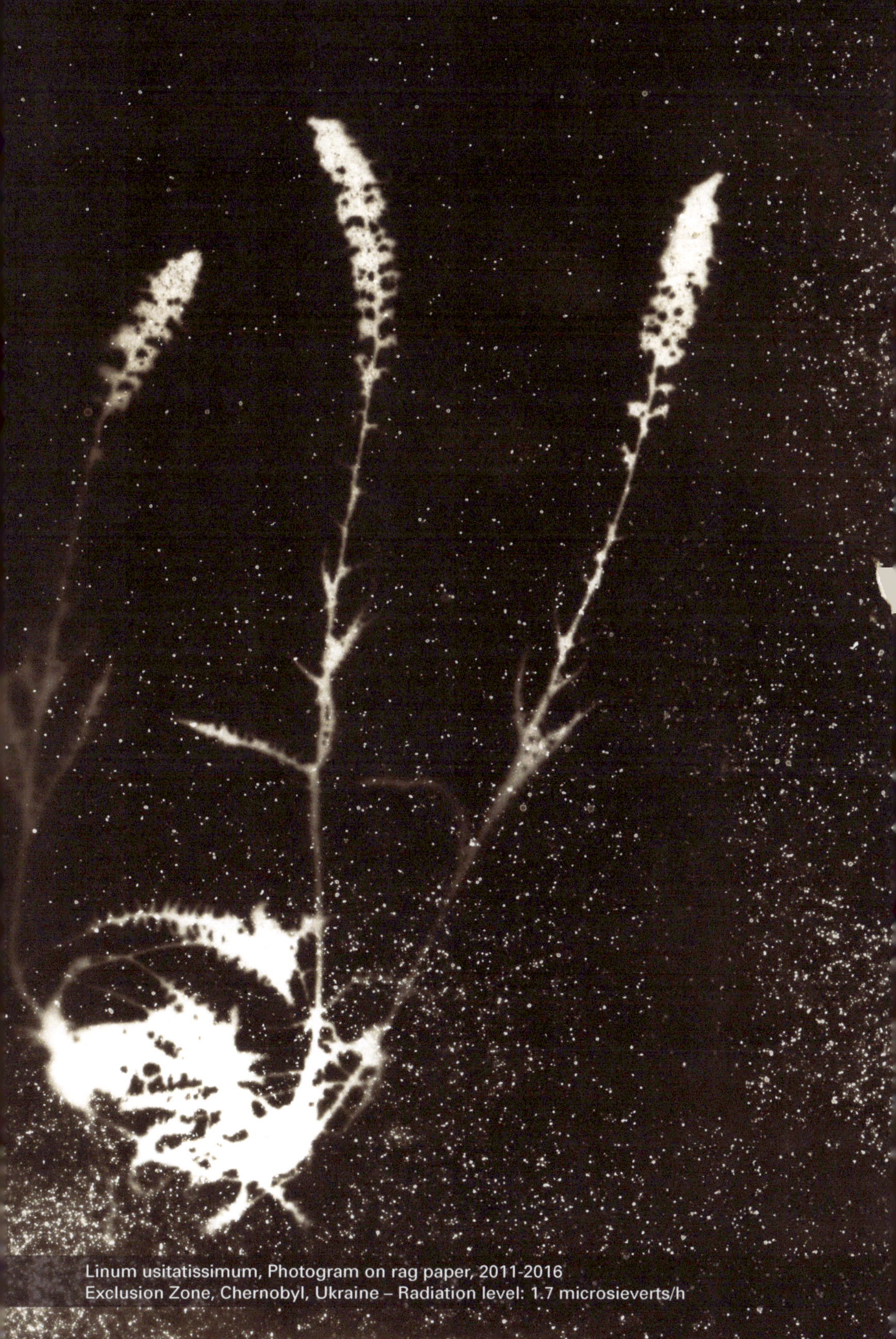

Linum usitatissimum, Photogram on rag paper, 2011-2016
Exclusion Zone, Chernobyl, Ukraine – Radiation level: 1.7 microsieverts/h

Fragment 17 **Fallout**

The extent of Chernobyl's fallout zone, which is significantly wider than "the exclusion zone," is unprecedented. The trail of radioactive particles stretched from Norway down to Turkey and from Russia to Italy and eastern France. It interfered with and invalidated our preconceived ideas about causality, responsibility, national sovereignty... In the broadest sense, *fallout* denotes the enduring negative effects of an action. Here, it has to do, rather than with a single action, with the sum total of human activity, marshaled by our attitude toward and treatment of the natural environment, our long-held views on energy, and our unthinking deployment of technology. The radioactive fallout from Chernobyl is the comet-end of the widespread fallout from the abuse of nature that no shelter and no sarcophagus will ever contain.

Now, a more specialized sense of the term combines the radioactive particles themselves, their drift through the atmosphere, and, when no longer airborne, their deposits on the ground and contamination of the soil and the crops. Fallout indicates dispersion, scatter, being strewn from a source, usually in the shapeless shape of dust. Still, the exact source is never clear: Is it what certain thinkers have labeled "the domination of nature"? Soviet irresponsibility (in Russian: *khalatnost'* or *bezalabernost'*)? The nuclear meltdown and explosion itself? The same is true for the fallout's effects, drawn out in time and space, dispersed, often-time untraceable to the origin. And all that is not to mention the dispersal, banishment, and exile of people from the exclusion zone, or the mass migratory flows that commenced as soon as the floodgates (or else, the Iron Curtain, unhinged by uranium) of the Soviet Union went down.

Nor was fallout of one type only, for it affected the land and its ecology, the people and their health, political and social institutions, moral and intellectual precepts, culture and agriculture. It sparked off external and internal exposure to radiation, which grazed our skin and which penetrated into us with every breath and every bite from a piece of contaminated food. The "outwardness" of fall*out* is never final. Invariably, it leads to incorporation, depositing radioactive elements in the body and its organs, in the earth and its layers, in the plant and its roots and leaves. But there is nothing dialectical in this succession of "safe" nuclear energy production, the release of radioactive waste, and its interiorisation in living organisms and their inorganic substratum. There is neither elevation nor progressive mediation nor domestication nor concrete spiritualization nor enabling negation in such a process that overshadows and destroys you from within. It is senseless, dumb, absurd. Like the very techno-culture that has unleashed it.

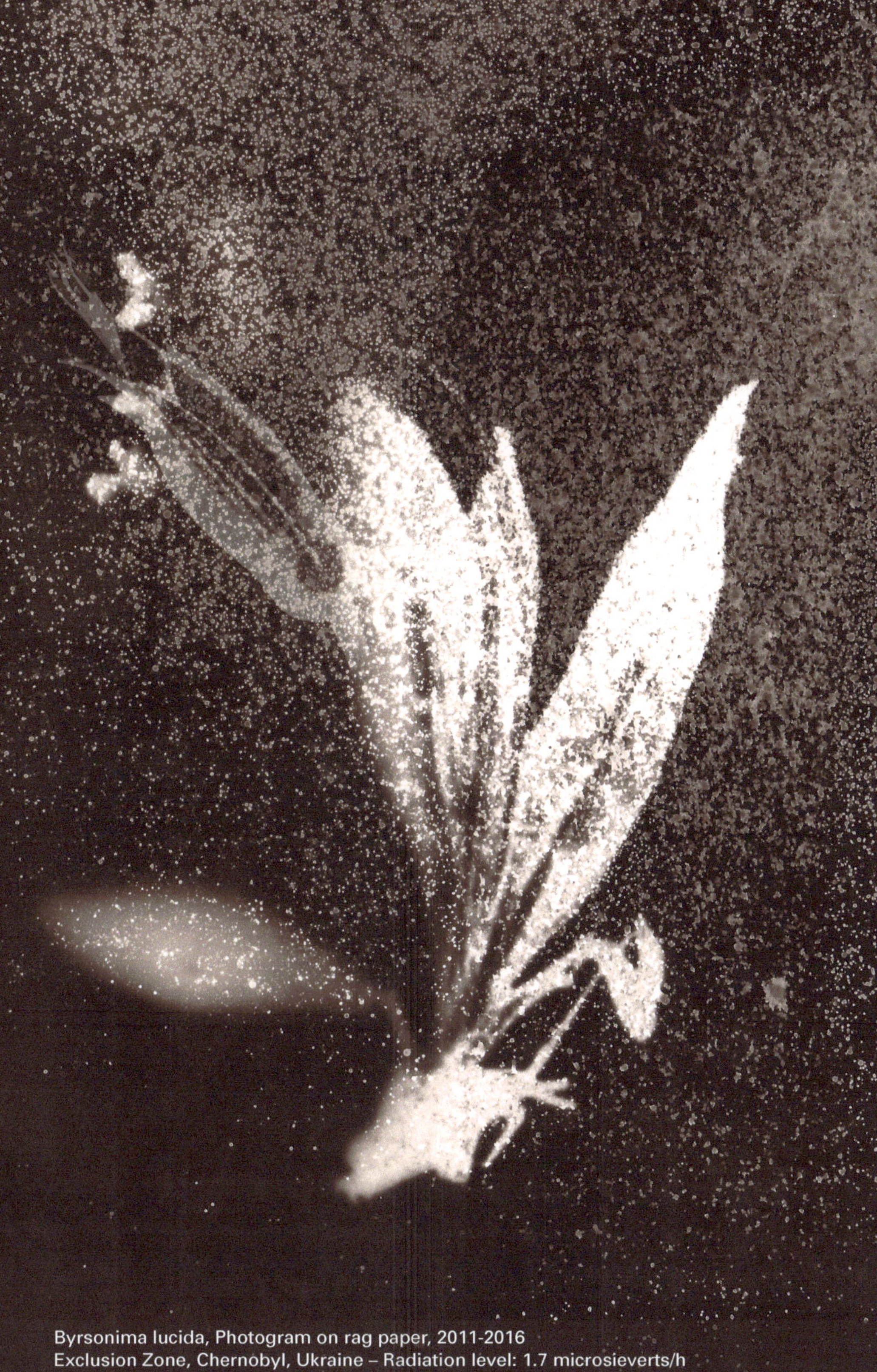

Byrsonima lucida, Photogram on rag paper, 2011-2016
Exclusion Zone, Chernobyl, Ukraine – Radiation level: 1.7 microsieverts/h

Fragment 18 **Back home**

I was back home in Moscow in the middle of June 1986, one week before my mother would give birth to my younger sibling. I recall feeling a little upset that no one seemed particularly excited to hear about my first experience of the sea or about the depressing state of local bookstores. "Chernobyl" was repeated like a mantra in every shred of conversation I caught: "Strong winds were sweeping through Moscow a few days after the explosion. They must have brought plenty of radiation from Chernobyl"; "The government betrayed us with regard to Chernobyl"; "Chernobyl is just the first harbinger; there will be others"; "Poor people; they had to leave everything behind"... The mood was that of a generalized, free-floating anxiety, which corresponded to an amorphous threat, simultaneously far and frighteningly near.

At times, it seems to me that I have never really come back home from that first outing to the sea. Or, that I have returned to a place, which was very different, more so than on any other Odyssean occasion. The maples and birches next to my apartment block were not barren as when I had left; they were already full of leaves. My brother about to be born. The adults deeply preoccupied. But, if I have not quite circled back home, then I am still (I have remained) somewhere close to Chernobyl, or, perhaps, it is Chernobyl that is close to me, as it, no doubt, is in my dreams.

~

December 1, 2015. While writing this text, I've dreamt that I am holding in my hands a pot with a blossoming plant, most likely a geranium, grown in Chernobyl's soil, very much like those from Anaïs's herbarium. I want to keep it, although I am also concerned about its radioactivity and wish to measure the levels of radiation before making the final decision. Do I espy myself in that plant?

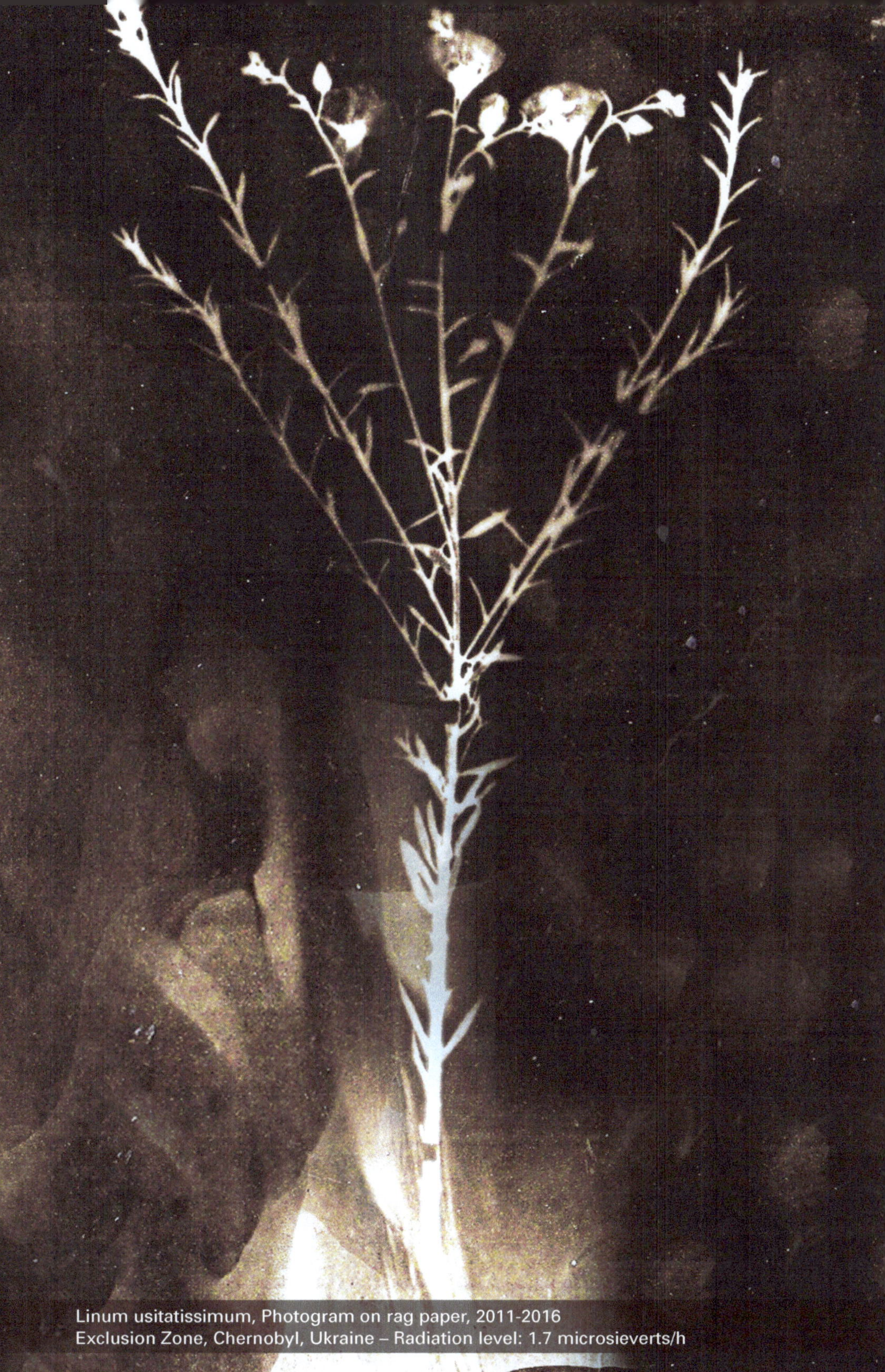

Linum usitatissimum, Photogram on rag paper, 2011-2016
Exclusion Zone, Chernobyl, Ukraine – Radiation level: 1.7 microsieverts/h

Fragment 19 **Can plants still point the way?**

We are not at home in the world after Chernobyl with its toxic mix of genocidal history and environmental destruction. Instead of being the masters of our milieu, we are lost on a planet transformed and mutilated as a consequence of human activity. Worse still, the internal compass, which was our consciousness, is shattered and no longer usable. We cannot even figure out whether we are lost at home or outside it, despite the reminder Pope Francis sent to us in his 2015 encyclical that the whole of the earth is our common, shared dwelling. Our glorious adaptation to any environment, ostensibly molded by the specimens of *Homo sapiens* according to our needs, has revealed itself as a spectacular non-adaptation, verging on self-destruction. Chernobyl is an indelible sign in this revelation.

To rephrase the question that gave the present fragment its title: When our consciousness has been exploded, can plants assist us in reconstituting it? Only on the condition that we acknowledge that they, also, have their own modes of awareness, sensibility, memory, learning and thinking. In a word, their own consciousness. Accepting the existence of something like a "vegetal subjectivity," we by the same token relativize human consciousness (in ruins) and let it assume its deflated place among other types of sentient and thinking life.

Vegetal processes, such as growth and decay, which Aristotle classified as varieties of movement, can also come to our assistance. Countering our metaphysically inflected economic and energetic delusions, plants teach us that there is no infinite growth, no growth without decay, itself the precondition for future growth. What the imperatives of market economy and the byproducts of nuclear power have in common is the suppression (indeed, the repression) of decay. This makes them incompatible with the world of the living, which they undermine and destroy. Against the background yearning for imperishability, plants point the way without leaving the places wherein their existence is embedded. They show how to grow and, by extension, how to decay better in our quotidian living practices as much as in our thinking.

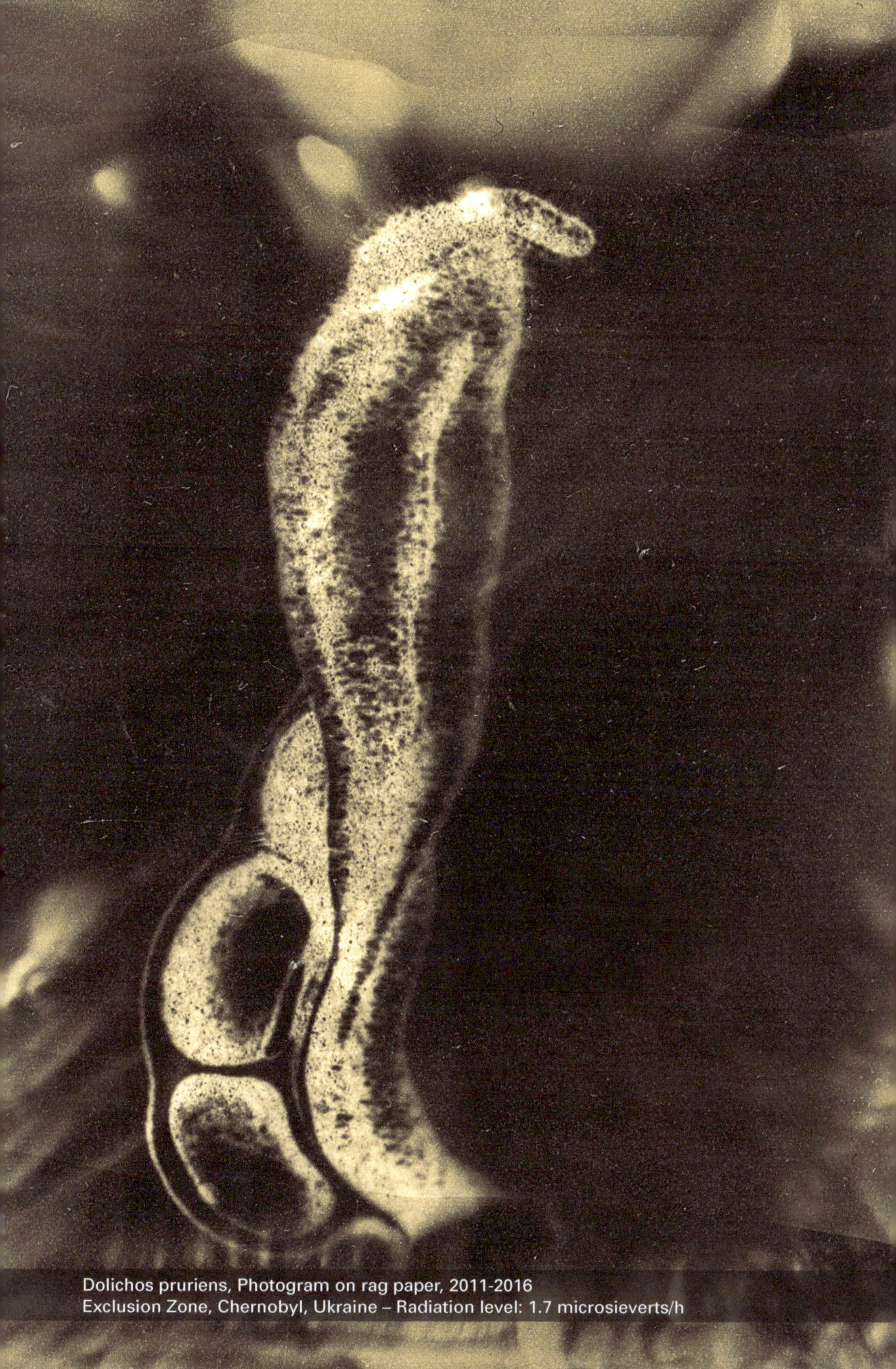

Dolichos pruriens, Photogram on rag paper, 2011-2016
Exclusion Zone, Chernobyl, Ukraine – Radiation level: 1.7 microsieverts/h

Fragment 20 **The Sarcophagus**

The Soviet response to the Chernobyl catastrophe was equally catastrophic, a prolongation of the perverse process, which came to a climax in the meltdown and release of nuclear waste. Sending (indeed, throwing) thousands of people to "liquidate" the consequences of the explosion, the authorities gave them surreal orders to "deactivate" houses, trees, and the affected layers of the soil by burying them inside the earth, something that Alexievich astutely deems to be "the new inhuman human task."[18] One of these endeavors is the Sarcophagus, the plans for which were hastily prepared while I was still in Anapa, on May 20, 1986. A metal-and-concrete containment structure for the damaged Reactor 4, it was meant to prevent radioactive materials from seeping into the ground and being liberated into the atmosphere. Among other things, it encases 180 tonnes of uranium and about 30 tonnes of radioactive dust.[19]

Far from "liquidating" the lethal effects of radiation, the Sarcophagus merely covers them over, and imperfectly so. It inherits the obsession with the concrete from the very technological failures it attempts to neutralize. The funereal insinuations of its original name must have sounded disconcerting to Soviet officials who rebranded it *Ob'yekt Ukrytiye*, "Object Sheltering," a designation that gave the impression of safety (sheltering) and control (an object, in relation to which we are the subjects in the driver's seat).

And yet, it was not the bureaucratic appellation but "the Sarcophagus" that was dead right. Humanity has been digging its own grave for quite a long time, which is, nonetheless, but a second in comparison to the terrible nuclear monument that will be erected upon it. Chernobyl gave us a glimpse of its concrete (discernible and made of *béton*) outlines. Encasement is entombment: together with radioactive waste, we are the ones on the inside of the Sarcophagus, even if it appears that we are outside. The Earth is turning into a collective grave, for the human and untold numbers of non-human species. Whatever the Sarcophagus covers, it cannot cover over the approach to the natural environment that has necessitated its construction.

The drama, and a tragedy at that, of contemporary humanity is that we are, at the same time, Creon and Antigone, the sovereign who disrespects ecological realities, burying alive the one who cares for them, and the suffering prisoner, deprived of the elements, of everything that makes life possible. The Sarcophagus is the stage prop and the denouement in this nuclear production, which is the enucleation of the subject. The subject is eaten up, self-cannibalized. In Greek, the composite word *sarx* + *phagos* says *flesh-eating*. Radiation and the techno-madness it metonymizes eat our flesh, eat into it. But there is more to it: the Sarcophagus is a Psychophagus, soul-eating. In this, it is akin to our notion of dwelling, which, rather than taking care not to impede the flows of energy through and around it (the school of *feng shui* is a notable exception here), circumscribes that which is appropriated through fences or walls, separation barriers and security perimeters, with the view to staving off exteriority and keeping the outside outside. What all these divisions enclose as property is, in the end, nothing but noxious waste, the waste or wasting of the body, the mind, and especially the body-mind.

Plants, for their part, break through concrete, growing in its cracks and upturning massive slabs with their roots. They open everything and everyone to the outside. As I noted in *Plant-Thinking*, "Unlike a crypt, supposed to keep (though it never lives up to its mission) its inhabitant in place, surrounded by inorganic matter, the grave covered by a flowerbed is always already opened, exceeding the domain of the earth and blurring the boundaries between life and death."[20] Plants will have been able to point out a new way. But what if, in the aftermath of Chernobyl over which the Sarcophagus presides, we have denied ourselves this simple, material, vegetal salvation as well? After all, rather than bury ourselves under a flowerbed, we have encrypted ourselves, body and soul, in the concrete.

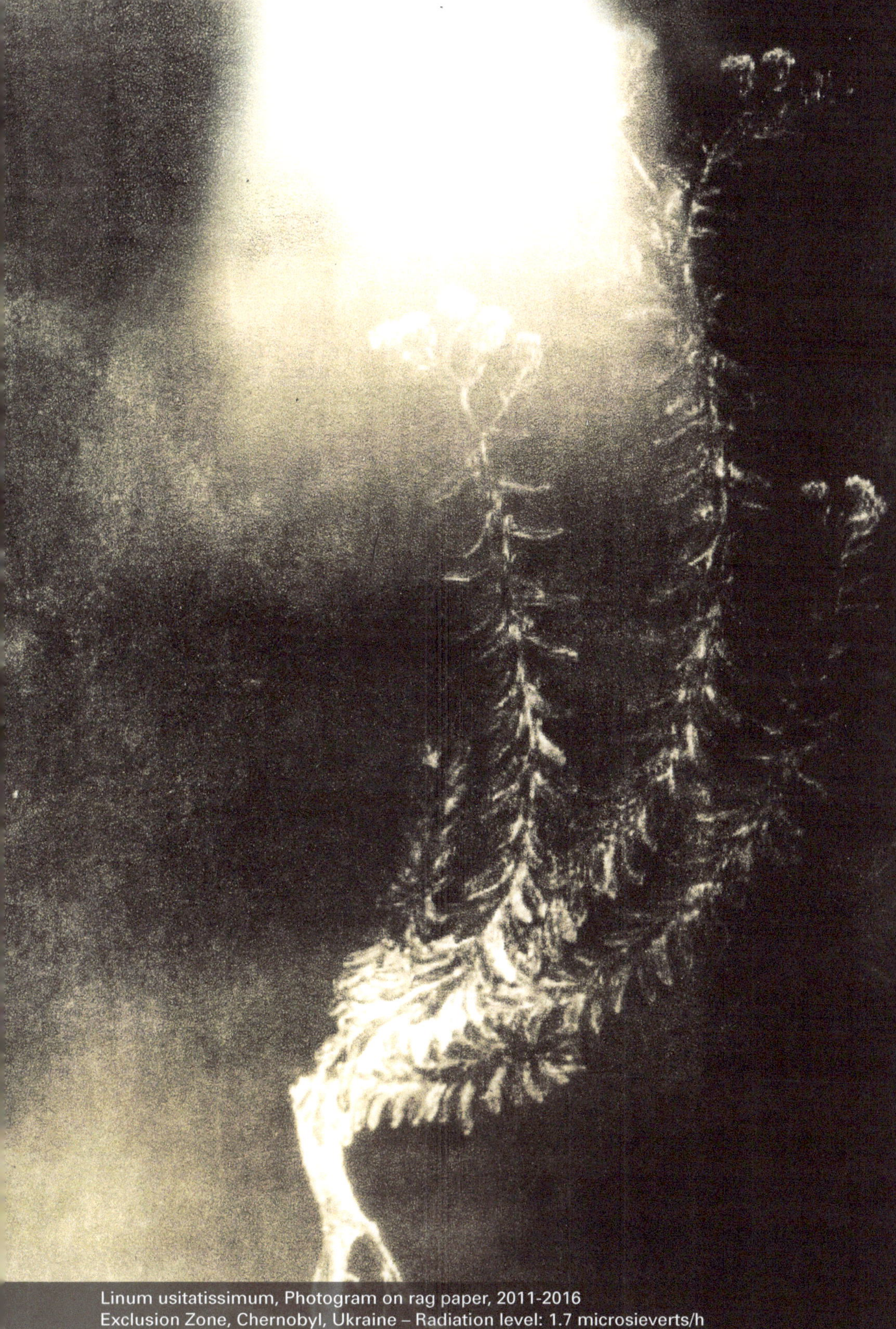

Linum usitatissimum, Photogram on rag paper, 2011-2016
Exclusion Zone, Chernobyl, Ukraine – Radiation level: 1.7 microsieverts/h

Fragment 21 **Anapa-Chernobyl**

Today, Anapa and Chernobyl are situated in two different countries, the Russian Federation and Ukraine, that are, more or less candidly, in a state of war with each other. There are, however, traces of the latter in the former—for instance, the radioactive elements that have settled in the soil and a stone slab, strategically put on the Square of Glory, at the corner of Revolution Avenue. The slab, featuring what looks like frozen flows of molten lava on its right-hand side, bears the inscription, "To the victims of Chernobyl, 1986-1996." The reason for this commemorative landmark is that, for several years, the Anapa sanatoria, including the one where I stayed in 1986, would receive the "children of Chernobyl" for rehabilitation. Despite its ongoing contamination, the role of Anapa was unaltered. It was to serve as a receptacle for the young victims of Soviet industrialism, be they a boy suffering from asthma in Moscow or the children from Gomel and Kiev, who received life-threatening doses of radiation. For me, the link between Anapa and Chernobyl is both physical and psychic. Physical, because my body has been exposed to radioactive particles from a locale I had never visited; psychic, because that unchosen and unregistered event requires lots of mental energy to deal with, work through, if not to make sense of or come to terms with. Readers already know that I sometimes journey from Anapa to Chernobyl in my dreams, virtually marking the actually unmarked trajectory, reversing its course but powerless to change anything in reality. The event of the thing: this thing that regards us...

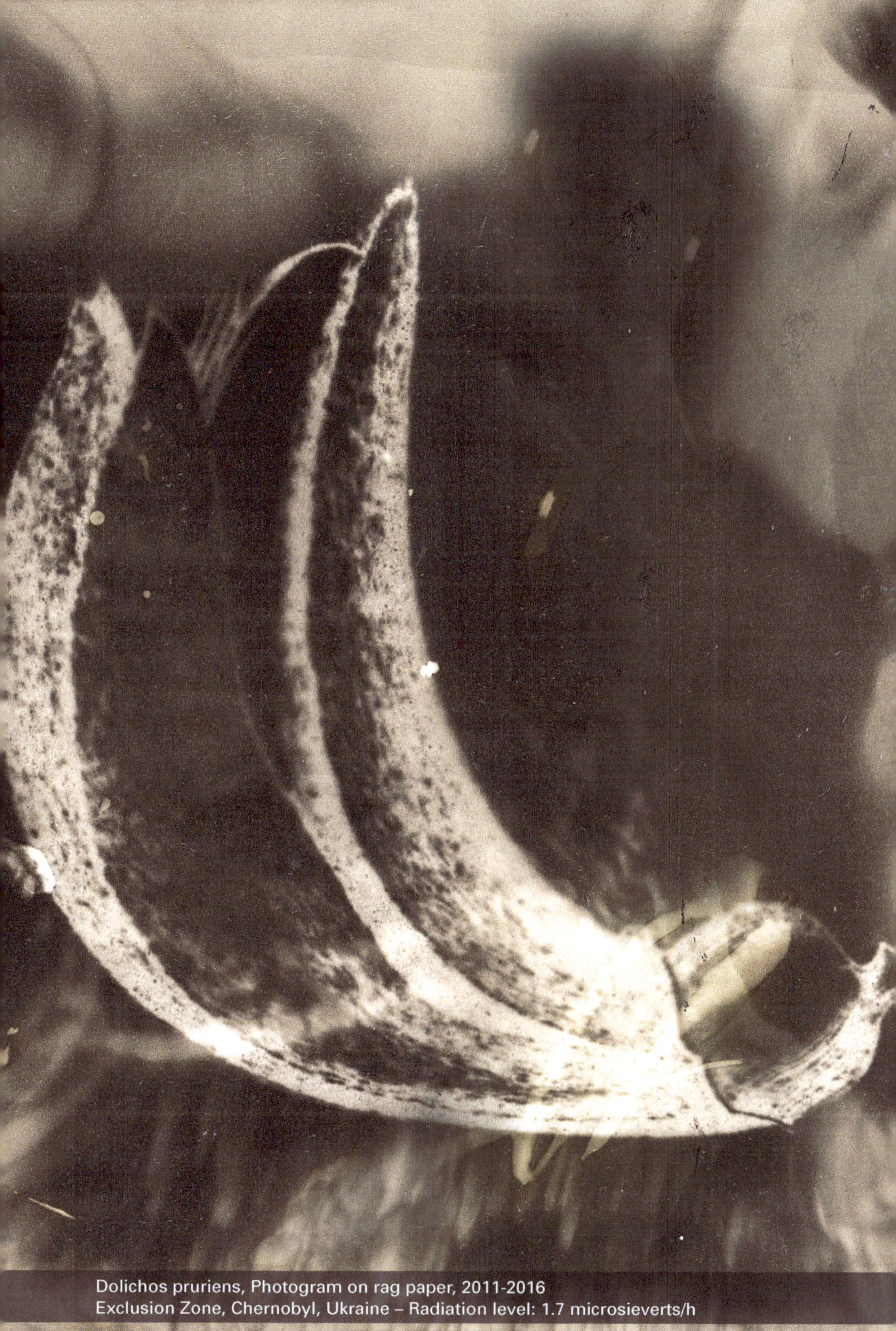

Dolichos pruriens, Photogram on rag paper, 2011-2016
Exclusion Zone, Chernobyl, Ukraine – Radiation level: 1.7 microsieverts/h

Fragment 22 **Exclusion zones and states of exception**

Chernobyl's exclusion zone refers to an area with the radius of thirty kilometers around the site of the nuclear power station. In Ukrainian and Russian, it is known more dramatically as *zona vidchuzhennya* and *zona otchuzhdeniya*, "the alienation zone." Often enough, it is called, in brief, "The Zone," *Zona*, which is, incidentally, the informal word for labor camps, especially those situated in Siberia, and, in particular, for the gulags. Whereas the zone of the prison contains human beings outside the confines of the law or of civilization as such, a radioactively contaminated zone closes itself off to and expels us. Bracketing this polar opposition with regard to the human, the two zones share the status of states of exception, where nothing is regularized, predictable, or normalized and where environmental and social emergency rules.

Alienation zone is a more accurate syntagm than *exclusion zone* for several reasons. First, it intimates to us that what remains, and will remain interminably, of Chernobyl is the outcome of a still incomplete process of human alienation from our environmental milieu, from everything that sustains life and that life sustains. Second, it indicates that the aliens are not some imaginary intruders from other planets, let alone inanimate objects or animals and plants. *We* are the aliens. The Zone is brimming with living beings, albeit not of the human variety. We, in our turn, have become other to life and have, until recently, worn this foreignness as a badge of honor, to the point of constructing our identity out of it. Third, and relatedly, the syntagm implies that the current state of affairs, whereby human beings are turning into the aliens of the earth they have ostensibly domesticated, is self-inflicted. Alienation is inevitably a self-alienation, for we cannot draw neat division lines between ourselves and our life-worlds.

The Zone bars human dwelling, but so does, through a different route, the pollution of the atmosphere with CO2 emissions. Chernobyl's thirty-kilometer radius is an advanced laboratory, at the leading edge of what is going on with the entire planet. In a consummation of the alienation or self-alienation that has unfortunately proved to be constitutive of the human, the whole world is on its way to becoming Chernobyl or a gulag. That is to say, the exception is gradually being transformed into the rule and the order of exclusion is undergoing an inversion. Entire regions of the world are converted into no-go areas, whether as a consequence of wars or environmental devastation. The effects of climate change leave no place unaffected. It no longer makes sense to single out exclusion zones (such as, at the extreme, that of Chernobyl) but to seek out the disappearing pockets of the earth still propitious to life, trying to inhabit them without resorting to the violence of appropriation, to maintain and to enlarge the livable realm both locally and through a global transition to the elemental sources of energy.

According to the political theory of Carl Schmitt, it is the sovereign who declares the state of exception and, in doing so, suspends the mundane workings of the law. The exception of Chernobyl, if it is one, does not obey this rule. On the contrary, Soviet officials resisted for as long as they could making any declarations and pretended that no deviations from "business as usual" had happened or been necessary. It would be too easy to explain their behavior away with reference to the general opaqueness of the regime. I want to suggest that something else underlies the irresponsible official response, namely the technological development of atomic weaponry and energy, which was, above all, a political watershed. Let us call this *the transfer of sovereignty to the atom*. Atomic sovereignty is the starkest form of our self-alienation, which gave rise to a power that is uncontrollable and that extends over a time span unfathomable to human beings. Henceforth, the state of exception will be declared wordlessly, in the language of the atom. Spoken pronouncements—still requisite to minimize the harmful effects of major technological accidents on those living in the affected areas—will be mere repetitions of what the fruit of our self-alienation declares by other means. Violently, atomic sovereignty puts language-as-word-and-speech, *logos*, into its place, reducing it to an insignificant exception from an overwhelming regime of silence.

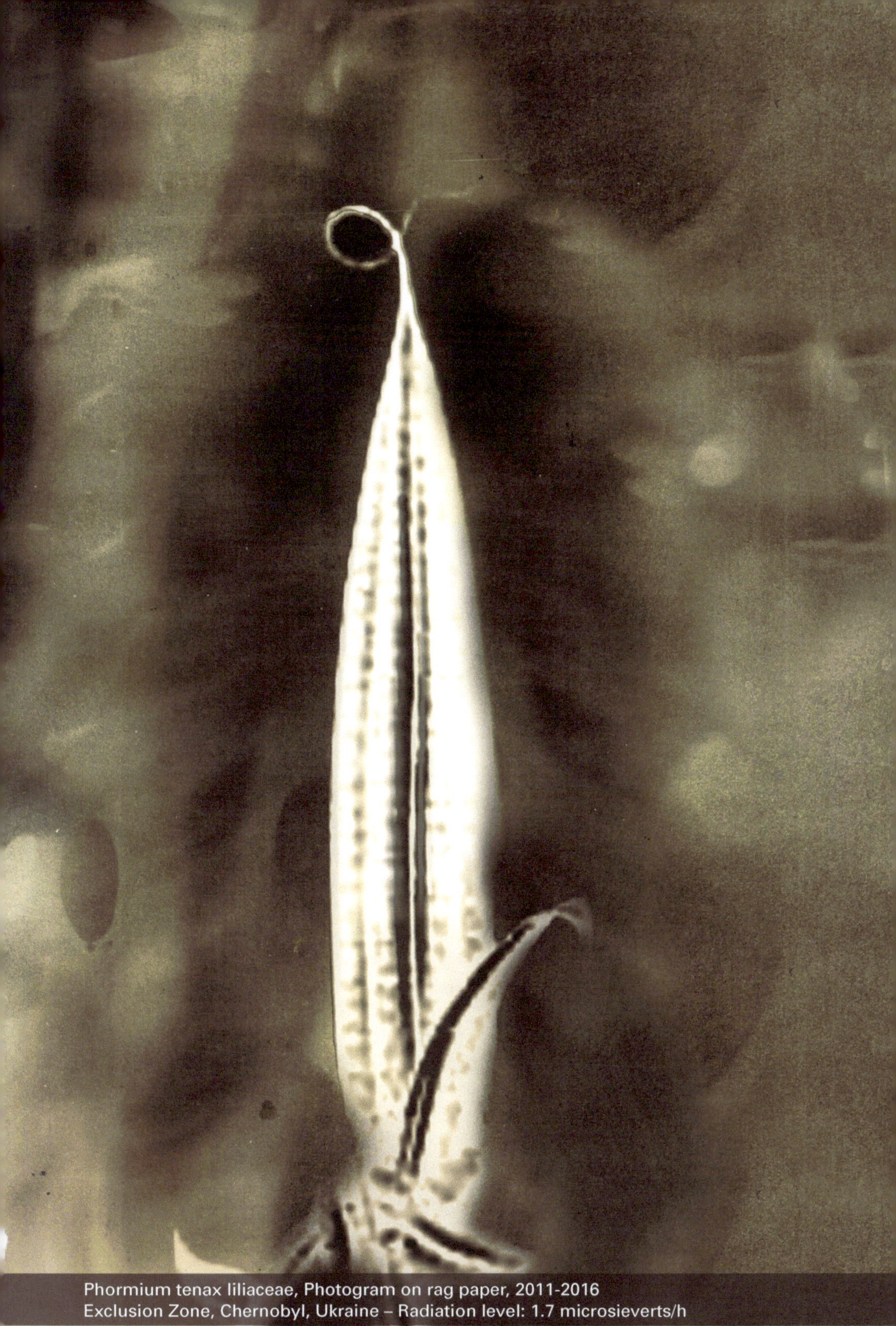

Phormium tenax liliaceae, Photogram on rag paper, 2011-2016
Exclusion Zone, Chernobyl, Ukraine – Radiation level: 1.7 microsieverts/h

Fragment 23 **Radioactive fire**

When I think about the half-life of U-238, tonnes of which are piled behind the walls of the Sarcophagus, the ground beneath my feet slips away and the temporal horizon recedes. Comparable only to the age of our planet, the billions of years uranium requires to release half of its radioactivity put it closer to eternity than to a time-bound reality. In this case, radioactive decay is distinct both from the transformative divestment of organic decomposition and from preservation, which keeps the same on the condition that it be impregnated with difference. Indistinguishable from its opposite, radioactive decay connotes stuckness, the indigestion of matter as well as that of the psyche. It does not stand alone: the spread of plastics, with which deserts and sea-beds are strewn alike, is another corollary to spiritual-material constipation, our lamentable non-biodegradability. (To clarify, I read *trauma* a synonym for mental indigestion. And, on more than one occasion, I have proposed that art and certain kinds of thinking may contribute toward our becoming "unstuck," obviously without changing anything in the physico-atomic reality of the half-lives characteristic of various elements.)

The invisible glow of radioactive matter is a fire devoid of the light and heat perceptible to us. Its burning, furthermore, borders on the eternal. As such, it is probably the closest approximation to the ideally inextinguishable blaze of metaphysics, itself predicated on the Judeo-Christian theological, divine incandescence. Just think back to God's apparition before Moses in the shape of a burning bush that did not burn to the ground, did not disintegrate into ash...

Across different traditions, East and West, fire has been construed as the physical force of ideality, capable of purifying matter. If the Aristotelian prototype for matter is *hylé*, or wood, then spirit sets itself to work as a blaze that consumes wooden materiality, elevates it in and as smoke, renders it ethereal. That, too, has been our view of energy extraction for millennia, until the advance of nuclear power.

Admittedly, with the splitting of the atom, the rationale of extractive-destructive energy has been intensified as science and technology penetrated and tore through the very core of matter. At the same time, barring an accident of the kind that shook Chernobyl and the world thirty years ago, the atomic flame has shed its finite and observable character, ridding itself of (almost) all material vestiges and temporal constraints. It seems to have brought to fruition the perennial fantasies of the inexhaustible unmoved mover and the Biblical burning bush, stamping living matter, as well, with another force, more subtle yet internally overpowering, one that affects their constitution all the way down to "life's program," the genetic code. *The uncanny fire does not merely analyze but molds matter.* It works on the living from without and from within, frequently with awful consequences for the organism or its progeny. Instead of destroying beings in a blazing instant of incineration, it prompts them slowly to annihilate themselves. This fate is, by the way, one that Creon inflicts on Antigone, who has no other choice but to take her own life in the cave, to which she is confined. The insidiousness of radioactive debris: its residual energy signifies counter-work, or anti-energy, insofar as those who have been touched by it are concerned.

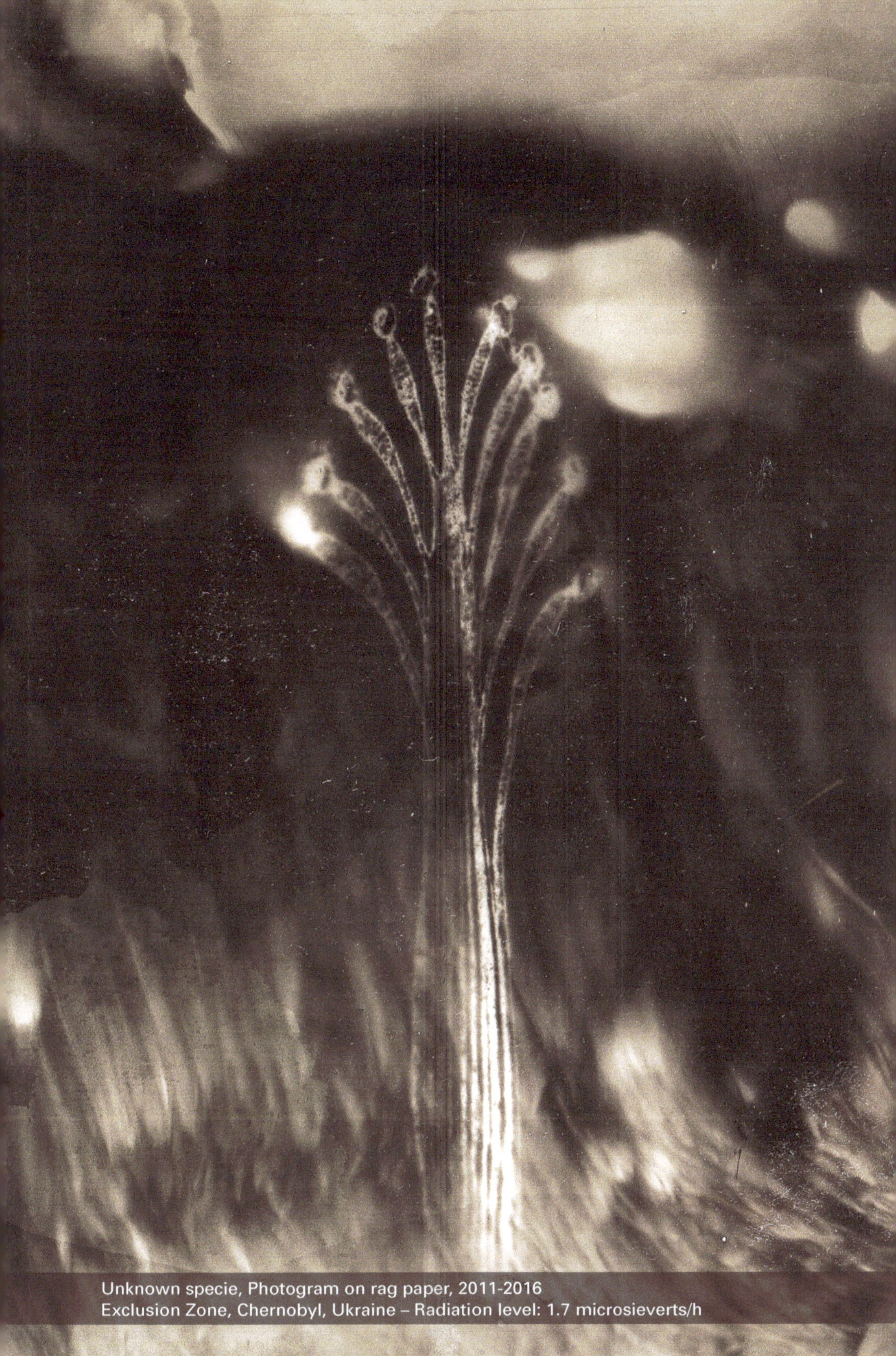

Unknown specie, Photogram on rag paper, 2011-2016
Exclusion Zone, Chernobyl, Ukraine – Radiation level: 1.7 microsieverts/h

Fragment 24 **A time capsule**

Pripyat' is stuck, a ghost city frozen in time. There, it is still, and will always be, April 1986. The Soviet Union has not yet folded upon itself; the drab and grey apartment blocks offer evidence of the uniform solution to the housing problem that imparted to the neighborhoods of Moscow, Baku, Riga, and Tbilisi the same impersonal character; the rusty Ferris wheel whispers what it remembers about the amusements of children who took rides in it and who will continue on this circular journey indefinitely, forever staying six years old.

Similar to pre-disaster reality, the disaster has never ended there, either. Everything mutely screams about it: the blackened clothes left to dry underneath apartment windows for decades, the empty streets, the libraries with books scattered on the floor. This silent scream of the things themselves cannot be stifled, even if, at times, Pripyat' River becomes the new Lethe. What do those who embark on "nuclear tourism" to the exclusion zone feel there? At what level do they forge a connection with this deeply traumatized time-place bespeaking traumatized and shattered bodies and mind?

(I understand, clearly, that a vast majority of tourists do not establish a meaningful connection to the places they tour but pass through them like the afternoon breeze. Pripyat', however, is not *any* place; it might not be a place at all insofar as its temporality and habitability have been irreparably disrupted. How does one pass through what does not pass, does not become a past? That is the question.)

Lest we be misled, eternal immutability is little more than a metaphysical daydream, notwithstanding the substantiation it receives from nuclear waste that eschews decay. Changeable beings *par excellence*, plants throw a challenge to metaphysics in Pripyat', where they are taking over urban spaces, and elsewhere. Defined by metamorphosis, they metamorphose the places where they grow and, if given free range, swallow up sidewalks and squares, buildings and roads. Not by chance, the new euphemism for the zone of alienation in Belarussia is "Polesie State Radioecological Reserve [*Zapovednik*]," which extends the language of conservationism to hopelessly contaminated and, therefore, "untouchable" terrains, alienated more thoroughly than before.[21] Plants will gently gag the silent scream of things. Where there was devastation and abandon, there will be a forest. That said, it is doubtful that the forests of Chernobyl would last, unless the insects and microorganisms that play a central role in the process of decay return and resume the decomposition of dead vegetal matter. If this does not happen, the mineral nutrients in the soil will be depleted, endangering future growth.

We might say that the herbarium is, likewise, a time capsule, keeping the shapes of vegetal matter that used to be alive and is now dry, brittle, fragile. A herbarium of lights and shadows, the Chernobyl Herbarium is, in turn, a phenomenological memento, a keepsake of impressions that supplant the formed matter of the plants themselves. It is a relic of a perceived instant, the silhouettes collected in it belonging neither to the surface that cast it nor to the viewer. Through her herbarium, Tondeur has succeeded in creating an intermediate space extricated from the contrast of change and immutability, a series of delicate moments on the verge of their disappearance. Her work with and on plants is a buffer between the mute scream of beings exposed to extreme radiation and its soft muffling by the (vegetal) life that goes on, moves on, survives. The photograms do not betray the trauma, the stuckness of the drive that prompts us to freeze the instant and be scorched in its eternal present, the never-ending high noon of unregistered experience. But neither do they revel in the traumatic stoppage, deepened or prolonged. If you attend to them with care, with a gaze which is not that of a visual tourist, they might give you a clue to a difficult, existential riddle: "How does one pass through what does not pass, does not become a past?"

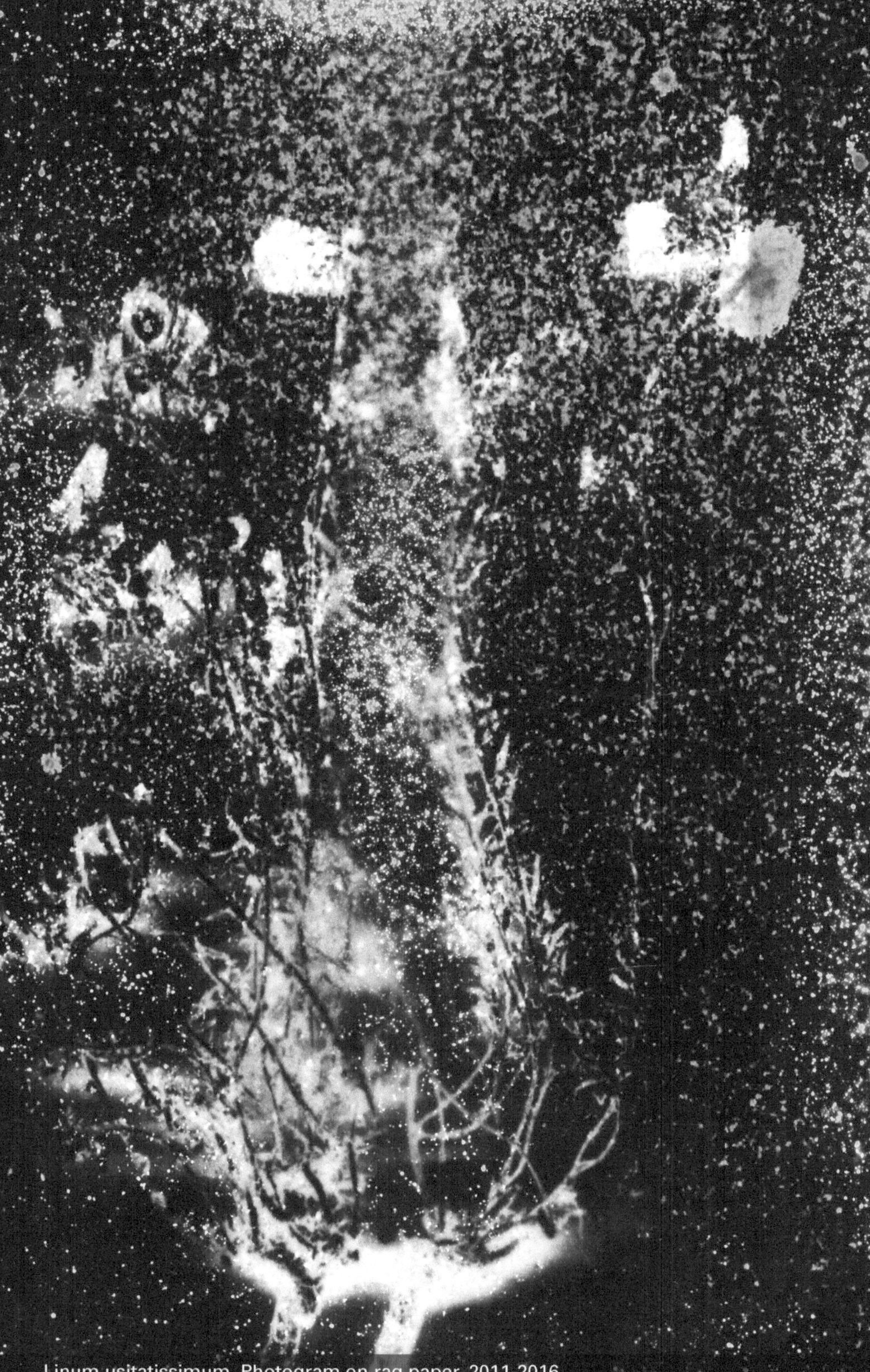

Linum usitatissimum, Photogram on rag paper, 2011-2016
Exclusion Zone, Chernobyl, Ukraine – Radiation level: 1.7 microsieverts/h

Fragment 25 *Abyssus abyssum invocat*

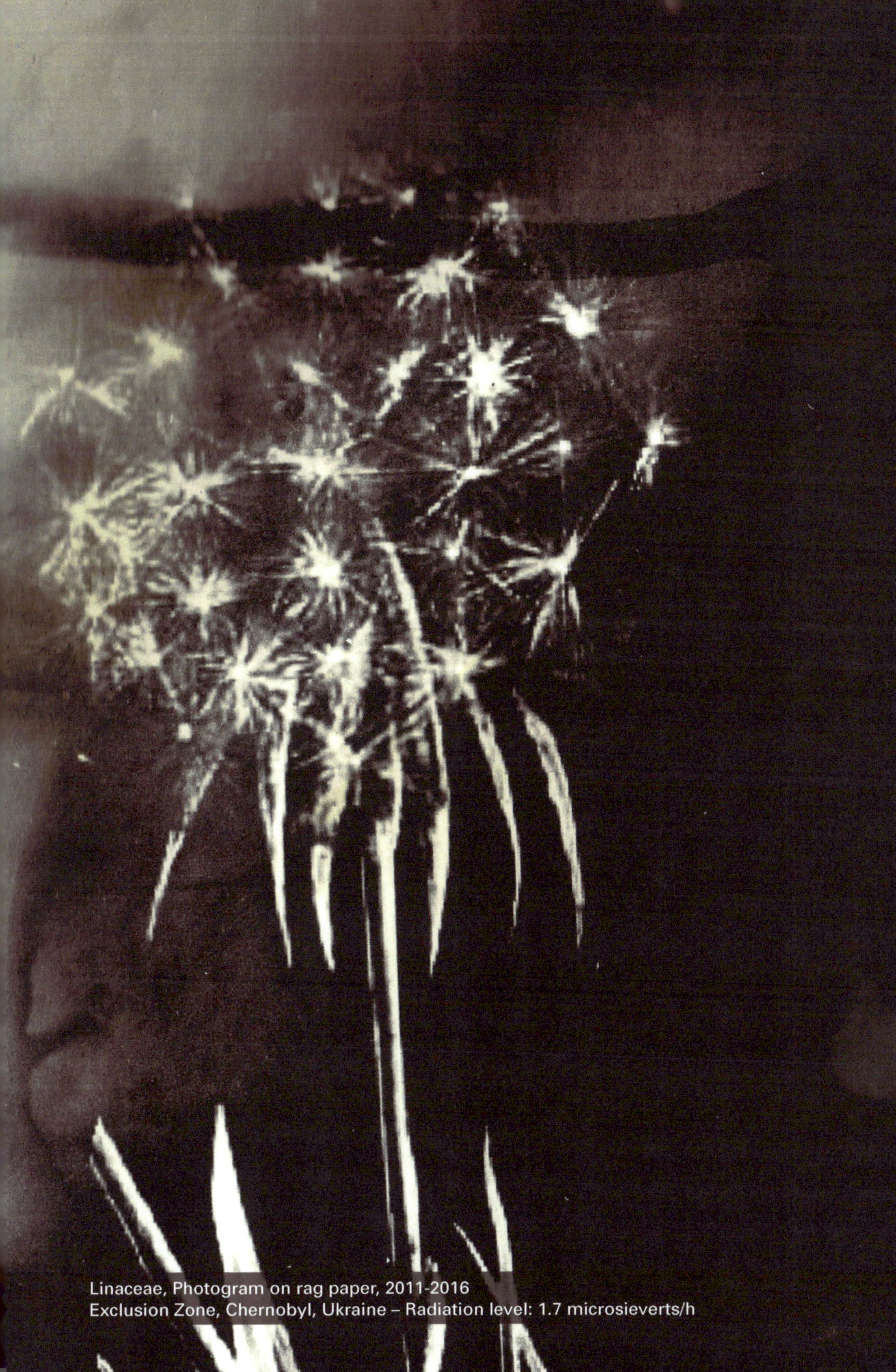

Linaceae, Photogram on rag paper, 2011-2016
Exclusion Zone, Chernobyl, Ukraine – Radiation level: 1.7 microsieverts/h

Fragment 26 **Recovering our senses… and our sense**

People who came into contact with extreme amounts of radiation report that their senses stopped providing them with information about the world. Photographer Igor Kostin temporarily lost his hearing when, flying over the ruins of Chernobyl's Reactor 4 so as to capture the site on film, he stuck his head out of the helicopter.[22] The levels of radiation were so high that all the photographs he took on that day were ruined, save for one. After a certain threshold is crossed, exposure shuts down the peripheral nervous system by inducing compressive soft tissue fibrosis.[23] You can no longer smell, taste, experience light touch…

If the senses create interfaces between our bodies-minds and the world, then their deactivation culminates in an autistic enclosure in oneself, being cut off from the outside. Again, the effects of radiation mimic those of metaphysics. In one way or another, both fashion a hermetically sealed interiority, whether it is a body confined in itself or a purely autonomous, independent, self-sufficient subject. Both suppress the body as an aesthetic receptor of *what is* or as a material extension of existence. And both shrink *the I* to nothing but abstract thought, the *cogito* stripped of all sensuous thinking.

Radioactivity is probably the most potent figure of metaphysics in our age. The struggle against nuclear proliferation, atomic energy, and metaphysical dictates is one and the same fight. It behooves us to recover the body as an object *and* a subject from its violent reduction to sheer objectivity, to a passive material substratum at the mercy of radiation and abstract spirit that arrogate to themselves the right to shape it at will. Since the early part of the twentieth century, phenomenology has been at the forefront of endeavors to reclaim the *gravitas* of corporeality. Adventures in vegetal philosophy show that this task cannot be limited to the liberation of human corporeality alone from the straightjackets of metaphysics and that the bodies of plants are also sentient, sensuously thinking, affecting and affected, open to the world.

The metaphysical-radioactive spiriting away of the body condemns pure "thought thinking itself" to a state of madness. There is no consciousness so long as it is conscious of nothing outside itself. At the same time, exteriority is not spatially remote from us, but is displaced and forgotten within. Reconnecting to it, we must come back to our senses from metaphysical and radioactive nightmares, the eternal conflagrations of which threaten to extinguish the glow of life itself. To come back to our senses means to awaken and, literally, to be reunited with the sensuous experience from which we have been expelled, to reenter our senses and to re-inhabit them. No abstract manifesto calling for a philosophical recuperation of bodies will do the trick. The retrieval of sense will happen only when we begin to think with our senses, to discern and engage with the sensuousness of other living beings (such as plants), and so to find ourselves, once again, in the world.

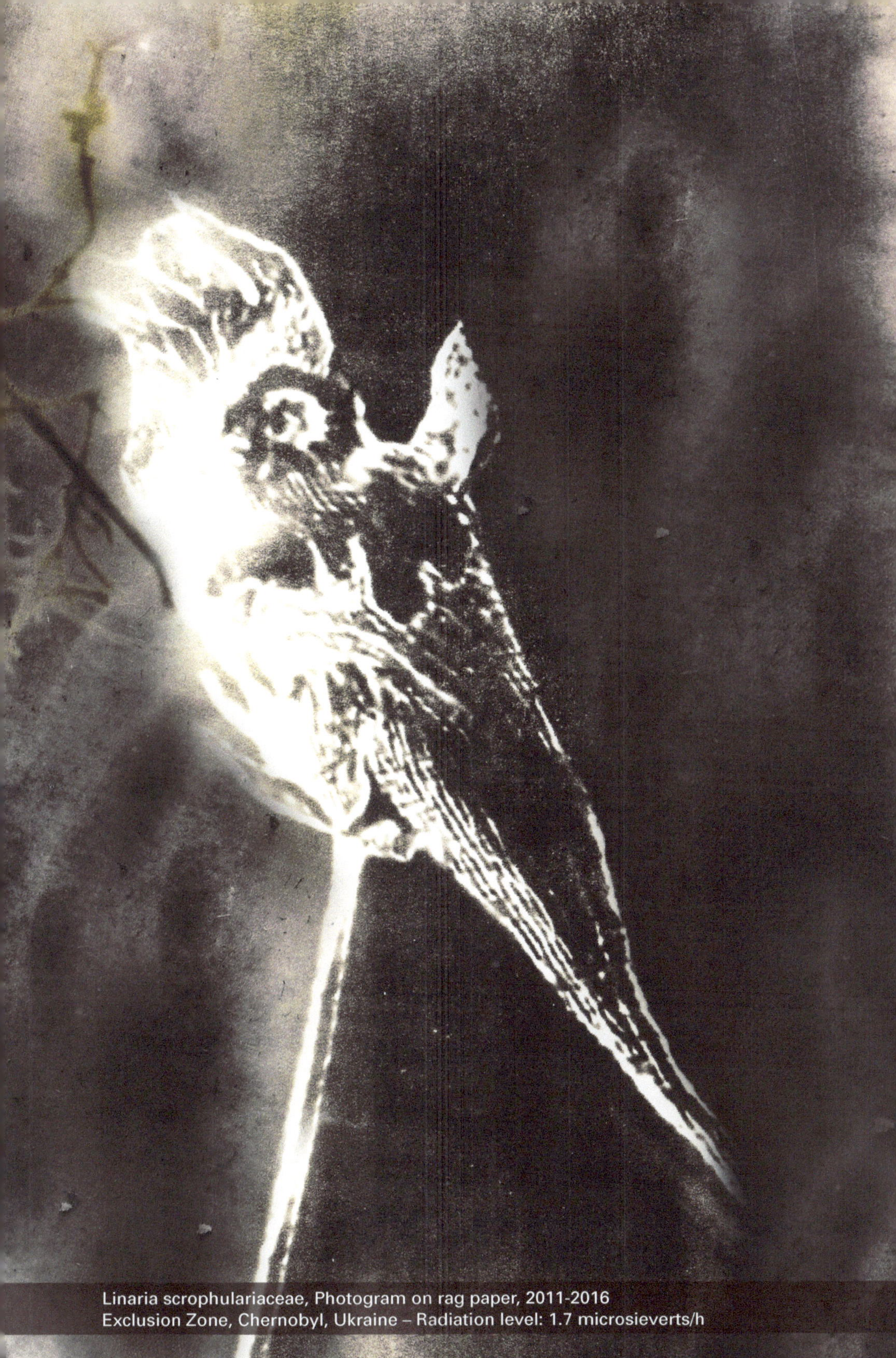

Linaria scrophulariaceae, Photogram on rag paper, 2011-2016
Exclusion Zone, Chernobyl, Ukraine – Radiation level: 1.7 microsieverts/h

Fragment 27 **After an end of the world**

Entertain as we might the secret or avowed hopes of recovering our senses and through them the world itself, the following conclusion is irrecusable: We live after the end of the world. Or, more accurately, after *an* end of the world. As I put it in *Energy Dreams*, "This is, finally, what *an end of the world* conveys: a thousand deaths (ends, times, terms, terminations, borders, or edges) awaiting our shared plane of existence [...]. The many ends of the same world imply a plurality of means, through which life could be destroyed, a variety of detours (as Freud liked to put it apropos of the death drive) leading to the same outcome."[24] In Chernobyl, one of these, in the words of my colleague, philosopher Susanna Lindberg, "technologies of the end of the world," was activated, put into action, realized. Reminiscing about the spectacle of soldiers and civilians ordered to bury trees, houses, and the upper crusts of the soil in the earth, the voices Alexievich ventriloquizes in her book are sharply aware of the apocalypse, to which they bear witness. "Is this the end of the world?" is a question persistently raised on its pages, now explicitly and now between the lines.

The world has ended, is ending in innumerable ways, and will keep ending for some time to come. So much so that it is defined by its relation to the end. Thoroughly finite, if not the very figure of finitude, the world *is* its ends. Considering, in the footsteps of Martin Heidegger, every human to be a world in and of itself, Derrida used to remark that every death was the end of a world—always unique, unrepeatable, irreplaceable. Endlessly worried about the finitude of finitude, twentieth century philosophy flirted with the possibility of banalizing the expression and, thereby, inoculating us against its disturbing force. Although something or someone did not survive one of the world's ends, survival was unflinchingly affirmed, often in the guise of mourning.

All that changes with regard to Chernobyl. An end of the world among others, it also portended another, more sinister prospect. In addition to terminating the actuality of multiple human and non-human worlds, the event of 1986 did away with the temporal horizon of existence, against which the world could still appear meaningful. It overshadowed (or, better, outshone) the light of meaning. Transcending the scale and order of time tailored to human measure, the persistence of certain kinds of contamination in the environment becomes unthinkable. That plants still grow in and animals return to Chernobyl, post-apocalyptically, does not disprove this thesis. Assuming that it is still plausible, the retrieval of sense will be belated, forever dwarfed by a senseless and unending disaster.

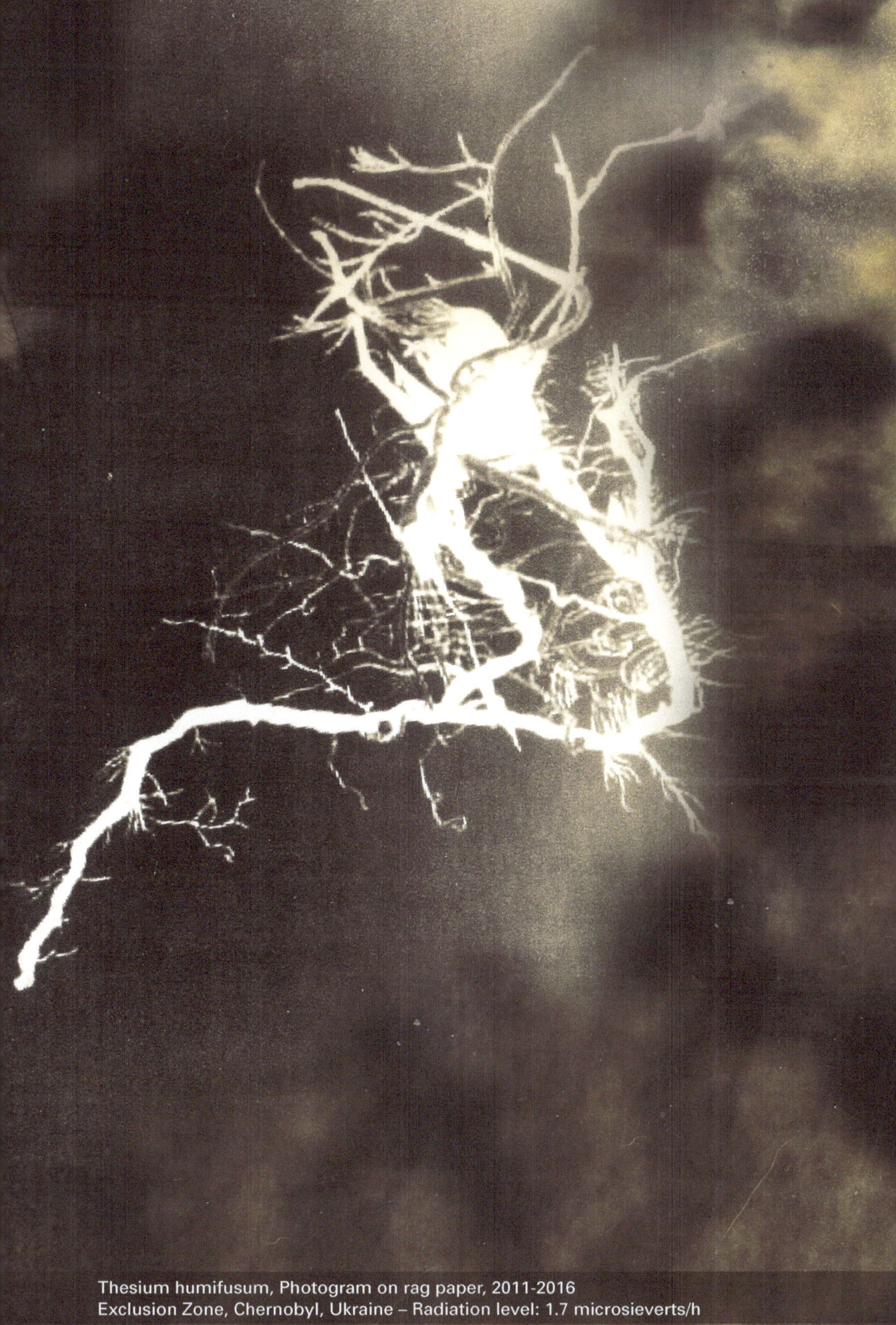

Thesium humifusum, Photogram on rag paper, 2011-2016
Exclusion Zone, Chernobyl, Ukraine – Radiation level: 1.7 microsieverts/h

Fragment 28 **Sublime beauty**

Chernobyl has made Immanuel Kant's aesthetic notion of *the dynamically sublime* obsolete. The sublimity of nature instills fear in the observer of a raging storm or the cliffs overhanging a sea. But, precisely because human beings are the more or less detached spectators of these phenomena, which overwhelm us by virtue of their physical force or height, we are confirmed in our judgment that reason is superior to the tumult of nature and that it is safe enough to contemplate this tumult, while deriving pleasure from the feeling of being protected in the face of horror. Not so in the case of a nuclear fallout. Radiation brings to naught our detachment from a threatening force and annihilates the independence of a viewing subject standing in opposition to a viewed object. Reason evinces its impotence. More than that, the imperceptible nature of radiation elevates it higher than the sublime. Absolute and free—in the sense of being untethered from any given source of danger—terror intrudes into our psychic lives. In the fallout zone, everything is dangerous, not only around but also within our bodies. We are not separate from the threatening reality, "caused" by and residing in us.

The liberation of the sublime from the banisters and barriers erected by reason allies it with "free beauty" that does not serve specific ends. It is this alliance that we find in Tondeur's Chernobyl series. The photograms do not represent anything. They only catalogue the traces of flowers, leaves, stems, and roots, along with the remnants of radiation trapped in them. The visual background effects are equally non-representational. Insofar as it suffuses the beautiful with the sublime, Tondeur's work is exquisitely attuned to the reverberations of Chernobyl in the aesthetic sphere. Her art does not imitate life; rather, it records life's vulnerability, amplified by the failure of reason to protect us, on the hither side of the beautiful/sublime divide.

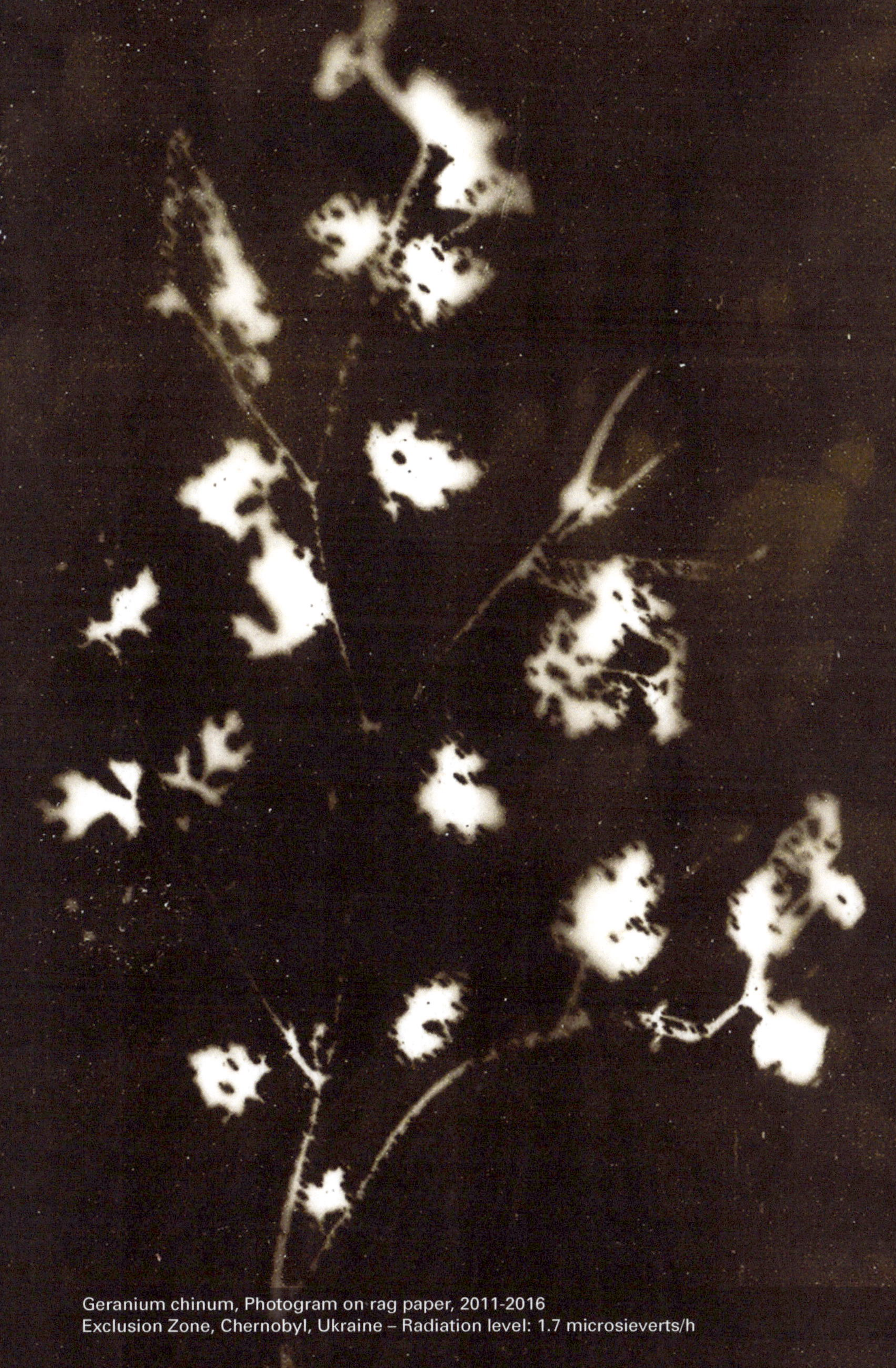

Geranium chinum, Photogram on rag paper, 2011-2016
Exclusion Zone, Chernobyl, Ukraine – Radiation level: 1.7 microsieverts/h

Fragment 29 **The dedication**

It would be only fair to say a few words about the dedication to this volume, written in three languages corresponding to the three countries most affected by the explosion of Chernobyl's Reactor 4: Russian, Ukrainian, and Belorussian. Translated into English, the inscription reads: "This book is dedicated to the earth, animals, water, people, air, and plants who (or that) have suffered as a result of the Chernobyl catastrophe."

Why not only to the human victims? Of course, neither the earth nor the plants nor the air will understand the dedication and will be oblivious to the book itself. But that, at any rate, was not my goal. I simply wanted to call attention to the fact that we do not acknowledge enough the effects and, above all, the ruinous side effects, of our technologies on the elements and on non-human forms of life, unless they prove useful to us. Not even the accent placed on biodiversity eludes the exigencies of utility. Conservationists wish to hold on to a wide, albeit quickly disappearing, variety of flora and fauna as though it were a living encyclopedia to keep in reserve, available for future consultation and potential utilization. That is why proposals crop up to create an extensive genetic database of life, permitting future human generations to resurrect an extinct species should the need to do so arise.

"But surely you do not mean that the earth, water, and plants have literally *suffered* from the Chernobyl disaster, or from anything else, for that matter?" an inquisitive reader will ask. "How can what is not endowed with a central nervous system suffer?" Let us tackle these objections by refusing to conflate suffering with pain. The root of suffering combines *pathos* and passivity, which may or may not be accompanied by patient endurance or passion. When I wrote above "What did our exposure amount to? Did it prepare the grounds for a trans-human solidarity?" I was conjuring a community predicated on the *pathos* and passivity of suffering, its outlines broadly sketched out in the dedication. On the path of radioactive debris, we were all plant- and soil-like, exposed physical extensions trapping some particles and letting others go through us, unwittingly. Far from a new dimension of our being, it is as old as our bodies themselves. What could be novel, in turn, is our attitude toward it and a reassessment of our place in the battered, fragile, inherently violable world, to which we belong.

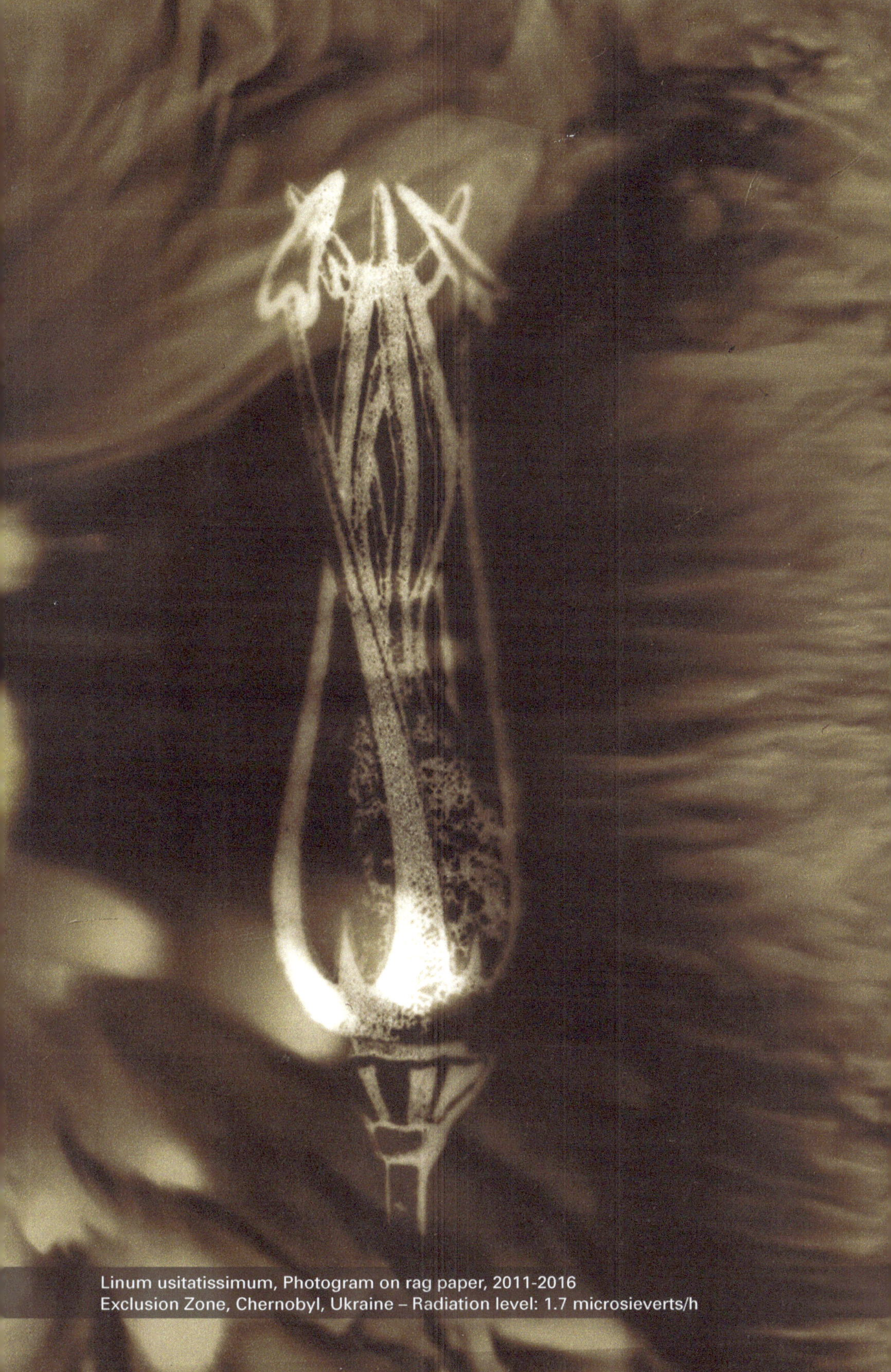

Linum usitatissimum, Photogram on rag paper, 2011-2016
Exclusion Zone, Chernobyl, Ukraine – Radiation level: 1.7 microsieverts/h

Fragment 30 **Half-life, half a life, halved life, life's (other) half**

- Whatever the reason, the number "30" presides over the time and the space of Chernobyl. It marks a grim anniversary, counts the years that had to pass for cesium-137 to release half of its radioactivity, measures the radius of the exclusion zone, weighs the tonnes of radioactive dust the Sarcophagus contains.
- Five-sixths is the fraction of my own life lived after Chernobyl, that is, after a certain end of the world, which had grazed me (how deeply?).
- A life divided in half, neither arithmetically nor geometrically. A break between before and after, there and here, then and now.
- For many, the event has halved their life expectancy and deprived them of half—in reality, of infinitely more than half—their lives, of the ground underneath their feet, their native land.
- The thirtieth fragment is half a fragment. And, paradoxically, still more intensely a fragment. The fragment's fragmentation. The falling apart and the fallout of the already incomplete.
- Life will not have been full. If it goes on, lives on, it does so only by way of survival: a life that is half a life, half unlivable. There is no such thing as a full life to begin with. But this does not make the mathematical guillotine of "half" any more bearable.
- Life's *other* half. Death? What happens after I find myself *nel mezzo del cammin di nostra vita*?[25] Life's other? Or another life? Remains to be seen.
- An infinite diminution where, simultaneously, nothing changes. Radioactive elements' half-lives will be halved as an equal amount of time elapses. This, too, will be halved, and so on: 30, 30, 30, 30: half, quarter, one-eighth, one-sixteenth… And what about the half-lives of 4.5 billion years?
- The diminution of noise emanating from what we call speech, voice, reason, *logos*. But language does not evaporate, does not vanish into thin air. Diminushh… Shh. Time to attend to the silent witnessing of plants and works of art.

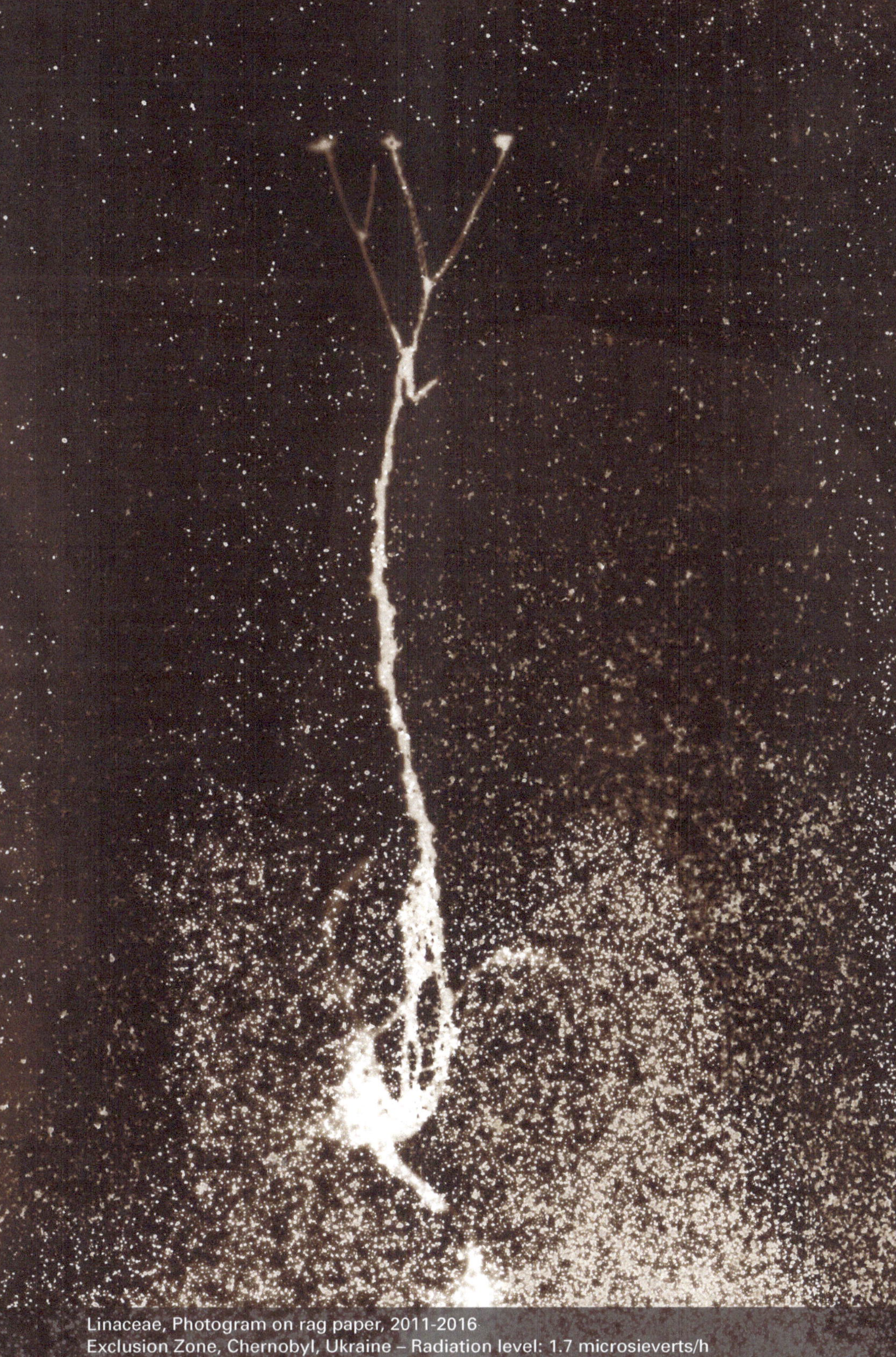

Linaceae, Photogram on rag paper, 2011-2016
Exclusion Zone, Chernobyl, Ukraine – Radiation level: 1.7 microsieverts/h

Postface 1

When I was a child I believed wars left the soil infertile. I had pictured the battlefields of the Persian Gulf War as lands where no more plants grew. At the opposite end, Chernobyl 30km exclusion zone is now revealing a ground where vegetation cannot die. Frozen in the present of the accident, the land comes to a standstill, fixed in place as in a photographic image. Trees do not decay. The silhouettes of plants are unchanged. Cesium-137 is at work. The mutation happens from the inside. Biogenetic studies on crops planted in the shade of the Chernobyl power station are revealing a subtle transformation, inaccessible to the naked eye. The core cells of the plants have undergone a transformation. It is not surprising that the Ukrainian population, exposed to high levels of radiation, has named it *the invisible enemy*. With the early tools of photography, I was drawn to explore the stigmata of Chernobyl's explosion on the flora. Capturing the silhouettes of these plants on photosensitive paper, I did not intend to represent the advent of an apocalypse but to interrogate the end of an era. Could these images called photograms or rayograms help us think, through the bodies of plants and the nuclear catastrophe in its etymological sense as an overturning, a disruption, of which Chernobyl is the sign?

Anaïs Tondeur

Postface 2

The text you have just finished reading is as much a book as it is a stage, a performative space of inscription, upon which everything has made its appearance, from portions of my biography to parts of plants, not to mention the themes and encoded titles of my books. The event of the thing, groundless existence, plant-thinking or plant-consciousness, the politics and metaphysics of fire, dust, energy dreams and nightmares have all been summoned to this stage. Unless it is not a stage but a vortex, sweeping thought and life into its midst. Between the competing paradigms of enacting existence on the surface and incorporating it into the depth, the reader will need to decide. At the end of the day, it could just as well be that the surface/depth distinction, so crucial to metaphysical operations, is itself folded into exposure (to radiation, thinking, the world, the other) with its external and internal modalities. If so, then exposure will have been a *pharmakon*, a poisoned gift of metaphysics that makes the donative source itself unravel. Do with it as you please.

Michael Marder

Notes

1. Svetlana Aleksievich, *Chernobyl'skaya Molitva: Khronika Buduschego* [translated into English under the title *Voices from Chernobyl*] (Moscow: Vremya, 2008), p. 49, translation mine.

2. Cf. Luce Irigaray & Michael Marder, *Through Vegetal Being: Two Philosophical Perspectives* (New York: Columbia University Press, forthcoming in 2016).

3. Alla A. Yaroshinskaya, *Chernobyl: Crime without Punishment* (New Brunswick & London: Transaction Publishers, 2011), p. 132.

4. Refer to Fragment 2.

5. Katarína Klubiová et al. "Soybeans Grown in the Chernobyl Area Produce Fertile Seeds that Have Increased Heavy Metal Resistance and Modified Carbon Metabolism," *PLoS ONE*, October 26, 2012. DOI: 10.1371/journal.pone.0048169.

6. Michael Marder, "The Sense of Seeds, or Seminal Events," *Environmental Philosophy*, April 2015, DOI: 10.5840/envirophil201542920.

7. Rachel Nuwer, "Forests Around Chernobyl Aren't Decaying Properly", *Smithsonian Magazine*, March 14, 2014 <http://www.smithsonianmag.com/science-nature/forests-around-chernobyl-arent-decaying-properly-180950075/?no-ist>. Last accessed on December 10, 2015.

8. Cf. Jacques Derrida, *Demeure: Fiction and Testimony*, translated by Elizabeth Rottenberg (Stanford: Stanford University Press, 2000).

9. For Ulrich Beck's conceptualization of "risk society," refer to *Risikogesellschaft: Auf dem Weg in eine andere Moderne* (Frankfurt am Main: Suhrkamp Verlag, 1986)—published in the year of the Chernobyl catastrophe.

10. Majia Holmer Nadesan, *Fukushima and the Privatization of Risk* (Basingstoke: Palgrave, 2013), p. 76.

11. Michael Marder, *The Philosopher's Plant: An Intellectual Herbarium* (New York: Columbia University Press, 2014).

12. Marder, *The Philosopher's Plant*, p. xvi.

13. Alexandra Cook, *Jean-Jacques Rousseau and Botany: The Salutary Science* (Oxford: Voltaire Foundation, Oxford University, 2012), p. 28.

14. Cook, *Jean-Jacques Rousseau and Botany*, p. 15.

15. M.H. Frere, et al. *The Behavior of Radioactive Fallout in Soils and Plants* (Washington, DC: National Academy of Sciences / National Research Council, 1963), p. 11.

16. Simon Dubnow & Israel Friedlaender, *History of the Jews in Russia and Poland.* Volume 1: *From the Beginning Until the Death of Alexander I* (Philadelphia: The Jewish Publication Society of America, 1916), p. 258.

17. Richard Evans, *Rereading German History: From Unification to Reunification, 1800-1996* (London & New York: Routledge, 1997), p. 155.

18. For firsthand accounts of these activities, see Aleksievich's *Chernobyl'skaya Molitva, passim.*

19. R.F Mould, *Chernobyl Record: The Definitive History of the Chernobyl Catastrophe* (Boca Raton, FL: CRC Press, 2000), pp. 126, 131.

20. Michael Marder, *Plant-Thinking: A Philosophy of Vegetal Life* (New York: Columbia University Press, 2013), p. 67.

21. Polesie State Radioecological Reserv, "Non-Fiscal Activity of PSRER" <http://www.zapovednik.by/en/Non_fiscal_activity/>. Last accessed on December 10, 2015. In a bizarre twist, Belorussian authorities could not resist the temptation to exploit the "Reserve" by breeding horses and pigs there, producing honey, and engaging in timber collection and processing.

22. Cf. Kostin's testimony in *The Russian Woodpecker* (2015), directed by Fedor Alexandrovich.

23. "Radiation Neuropathy," in *Merritt's Neurology*, Twelfth Edition, edited by Lewis Rowland and Timothy Pedley (Philadelphia: Kluwer, 2010), p. 833.

24. Michael Marder, *Energy Dreams* (New York: Columbia University Press, forthcoming in 2017).

25. This is a reference to the first line of Dante's *Divine Comedy*: "In the middle of our life's path..."

www.ingramcontent.com/pod-product-compliance
Lightning Source LLC
LaVergne TN
LVHW052257100826
845147LV00001B/71

* 9 7 8 1 7 8 5 4 2 0 2 6 9 *